THE WORLD BOOK

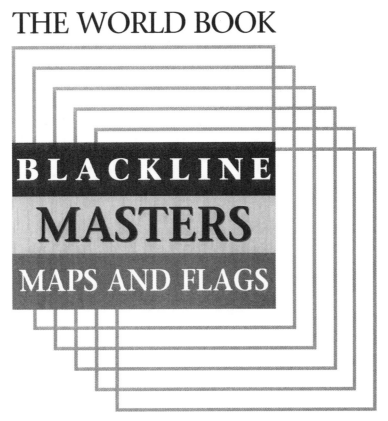

BLACKLINE
MASTERS
MAPS AND FLAGS

FOR STATES AND PROVINCES

Editorial: Shawn Brennan, Jeanne Johnson, Maureen Liebenson
Cartography: Don Minnick, Wayne Pichler
Art and Design: John Horvath, Wilma Stevens
Production: Kathe Ellefsen, Madelyn Underwood
Proofreading: Anne Dillon, Chad Rubel
Manufacturing: Marco Morales

For information on other World Book products,
call 1-800-WORLDBK (967-5325), or visit our
Web site at **http://www.worldbook.com**.

World Book, Inc.
233 N. Michigan Ave.
Chicago, IL 60601

ISBN 0-7166-7407-6

Printed in the United States of America
  3 4 5 6 7 8 9 06 05 04 03 02

Table of Contents

United

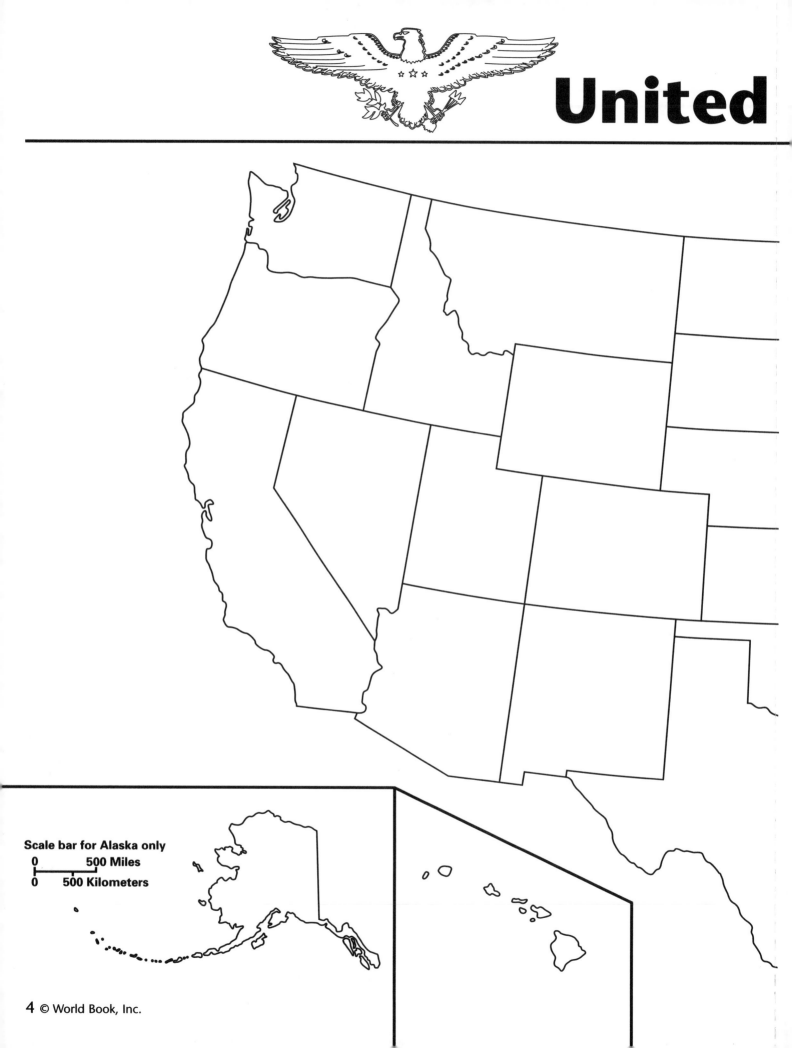

States of America

"In God We Trust"

Washington,
D.C.

North

Scale bar for all states except Alaska

0   500 Miles

0   500 Kilometers

5

U.S. Facts and Symbols

The United States flag includes 13 red and white stripes. In the upper-left corner are 50 white stars on a blue background. The stripes represent the original Thirteen Colonies. The stars represent the 50 U.S. states.

The bald eagle, a symbol of freedom and power, is found only in North America and is the national bird of the United States.

The Great Seal shows the bald eagle holding an olive branch and arrows, symbolizing a desire for peace but the ability to wage war. The reverse side bears the Eye of Providence, representing God, and a pyramid dated 1776, the year the U.S. declared its independence.

The United States of America is the third largest country in the world in population and the fourth largest in area.

The United States consists of 50 states and the District of Columbia. The District of Columbia is a piece of land set aside by the federal government for the nation's capital. The city of Washington covers the entire District.

Front side of the Great Seal

Reverse side of the Great Seal

7

State Facts

State	Area in sq. mi.	Area in sq. km	Admitted to the Union
Alabama	51,718	133,950	1819
Alaska	587,878	1,522,596	1959
Arizona	114,007	295,276	1912
Arkansas	53,183	137,742	1836
California	158,648	410,896	1850
Colorado	104,100	269,618	1876
Connecticut	5,006	12,966	1788
Delaware	2,026	5,246	1787
Florida	58,681	151,982	1845
Georgia	58,930	152,627	1788
Hawaii	6,459	16,729	1959
Idaho	83,574	216,456	1890
Illinois	56,343	145,928	1818
Indiana	36,185	93,720	1816
Iowa	56,276	145,754	1846
Kansas	82,282	213,110	1861
Kentucky	40,411	104,665	1792
Louisiana	47,717	123,586	1812
Maine	33,128	85,801	1820
Maryland	10,455	27,077	1788
Massachusetts	8,262	21,398	1788
Michigan	58,513	151,548	1837
Minnesota	84,397	218,587	1858
Mississippi	47,695	123,530	1817
Missouri	69,709	180,546	1821

State	Area in sq. mi.	Area in sq. km	Admitted to the Union
Montana	147,047	380,849	1889
Nebraska	77,359	200,358	1867
Nevada	110,567	286,367	1864
New Hampshire	9,283	24,044	1788
New Jersey	7,790	20,175	1787
New Mexico	121,599	314,939	1912
New York	49,112	127,200	1788
North Carolina	52,672	136,421	1789
North Dakota	70,704	183,123	1889
Ohio	41,328	107,040	1803
Oklahoma	69,903	181,048	1907
Oregon	97,052	251,365	1859
Pennsylvania	45,310	117,351	1787
Rhode Island	1,213	3,142	1790
South Carolina	31,117	80,593	1788
South Dakota	77,122	199,744	1889
Tennessee	42,146	109,158	1796
Texas	266,874	691,201	1845
Utah	84,905	219,902	1896
Vermont	9,615	24,903	1791
Virginia	40,598	105,149	1788
Washington	68,126	176,446	1889
West Virginia	24,231	62,759	1863
Wisconsin	56,145	145,414	1848
Wyoming	97,818	253,349	1890

Alabama

"We Dare Defend Our Rights"

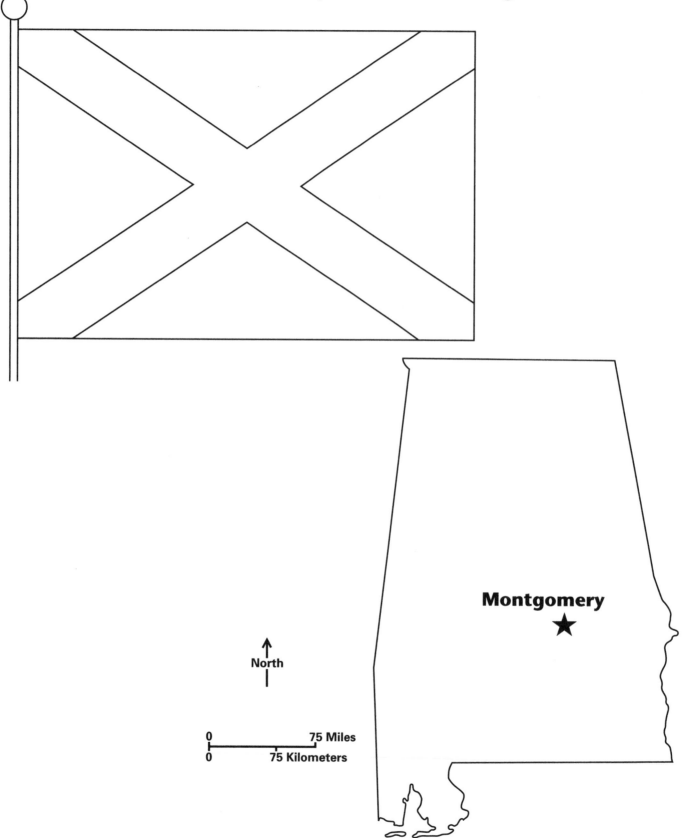

Montgomery

North

| 0 | 75 Miles |
| 0 | 75 Kilometers |

Alaska

"North to the Future"

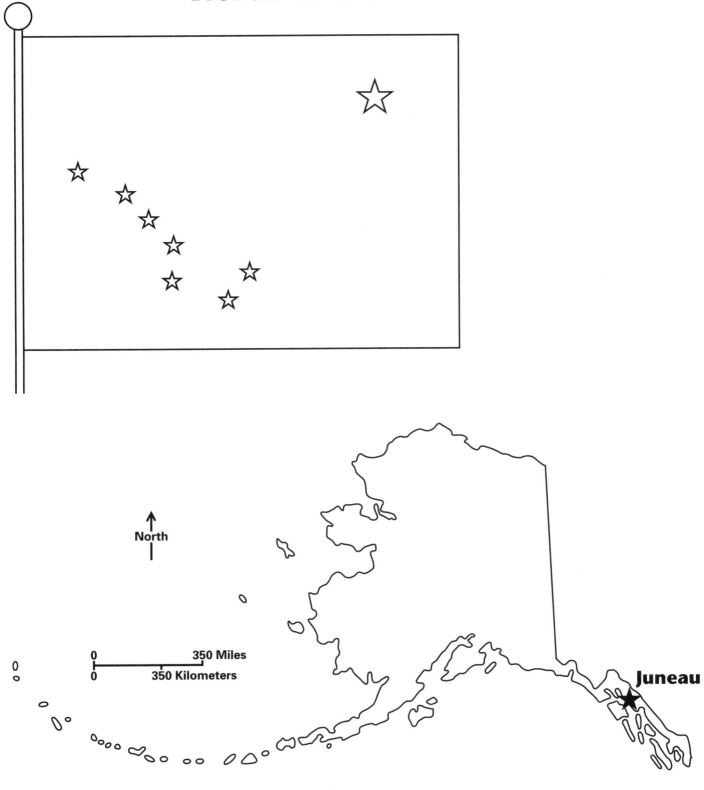

North

0   350 Miles
0   350 Kilometers

Juneau

Arizona

"God Enriches"

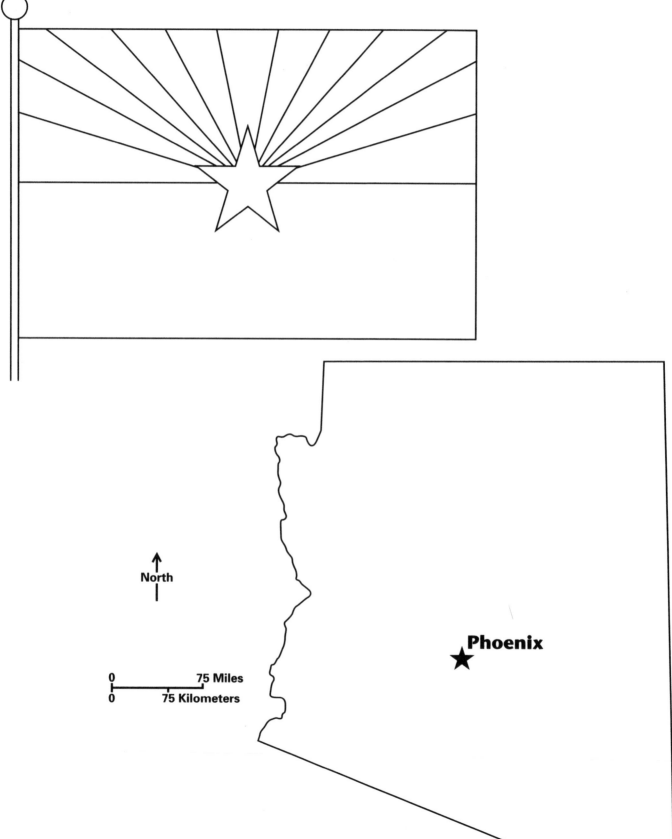

North

Phoenix

0   75 Miles
0   75 Kilometers

Arkansas

"The People Rule"

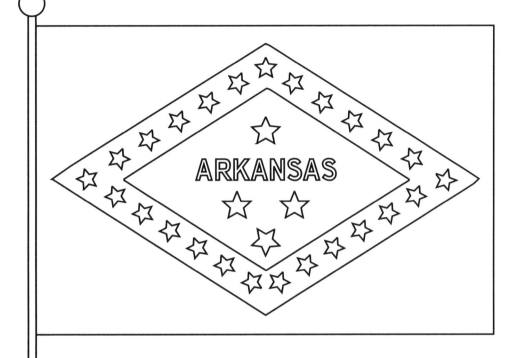

Little Rock
★

North

0   50 Miles
0   50 Kilometers

California

"I Have Found It"

CALIFORNIA REPUBLIC

★ **Sacramento**

North

| 0 | 100 Miles |
| 0 | 100 Kilometers |

Colorado

"Nothing Without Providence"

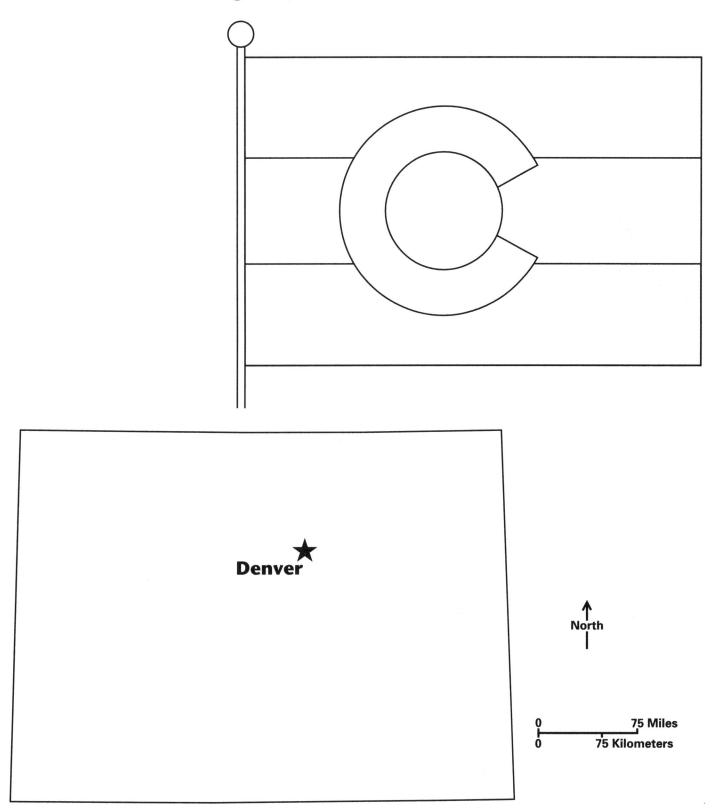

Denver ★

North

0   75 Miles
0   75 Kilometers

Connecticut

"He Who Transplanted Still Sustains"

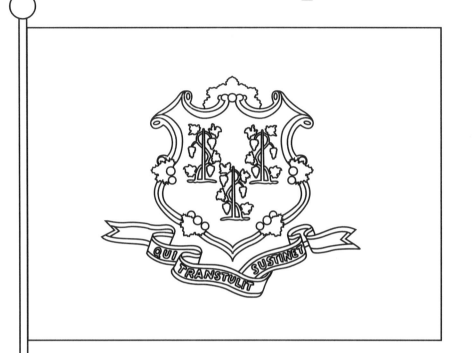

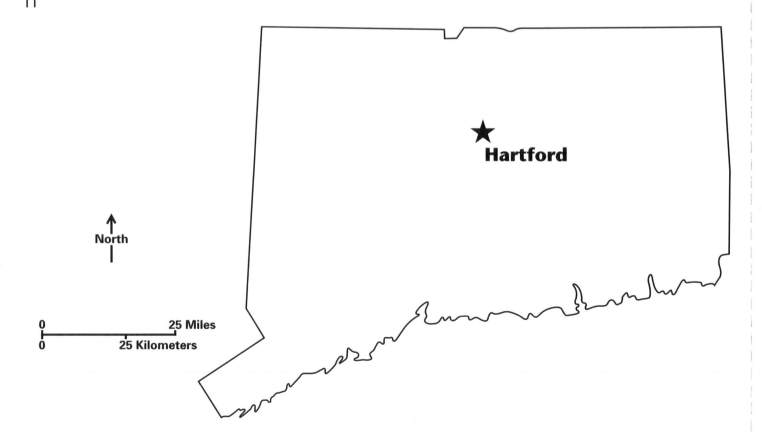

★
Hartford

North

0   25 Miles
0   25 Kilometers

Delaware

"Liberty and Independence"

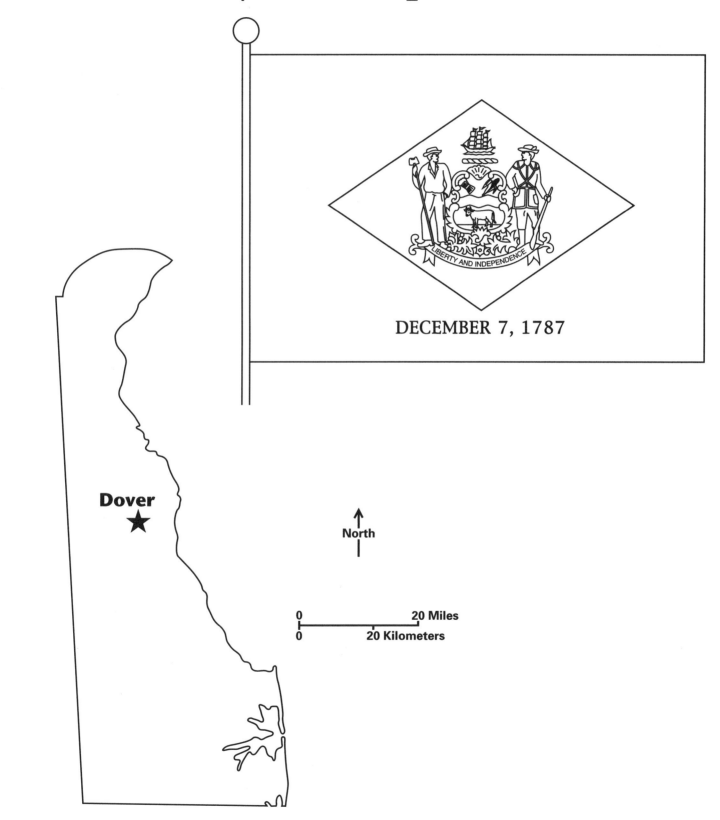

DECEMBER 7, 1787

Dover
★

North

0   **20 Miles**
0   **20 Kilometers**

Florida

"In God We Trust"

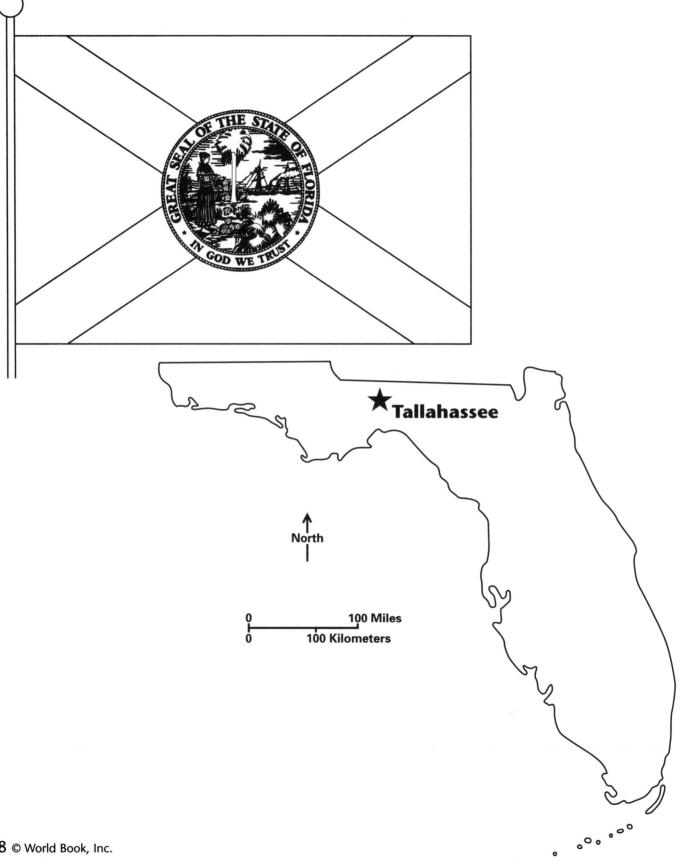

★ **Tallahassee**

↑
North

0   100 Miles
0   100 Kilometers

Georgia

"Wisdom, Justice, and Moderation"

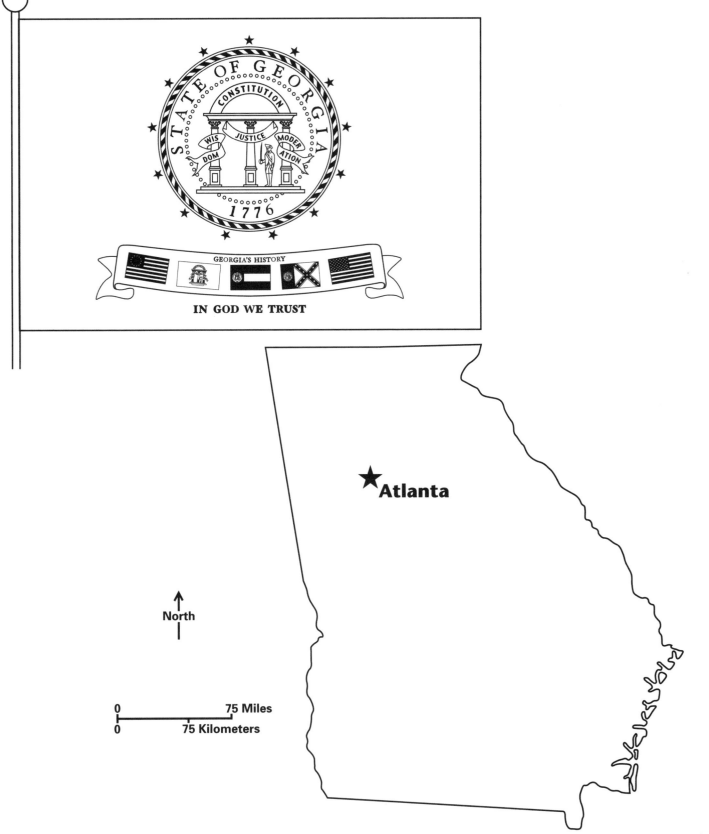

★**Atlanta**

↑
North

0   75 Miles
0   75 Kilometers

Hawaii

"The Life of the Land Is Perpetuated in Righteousness"

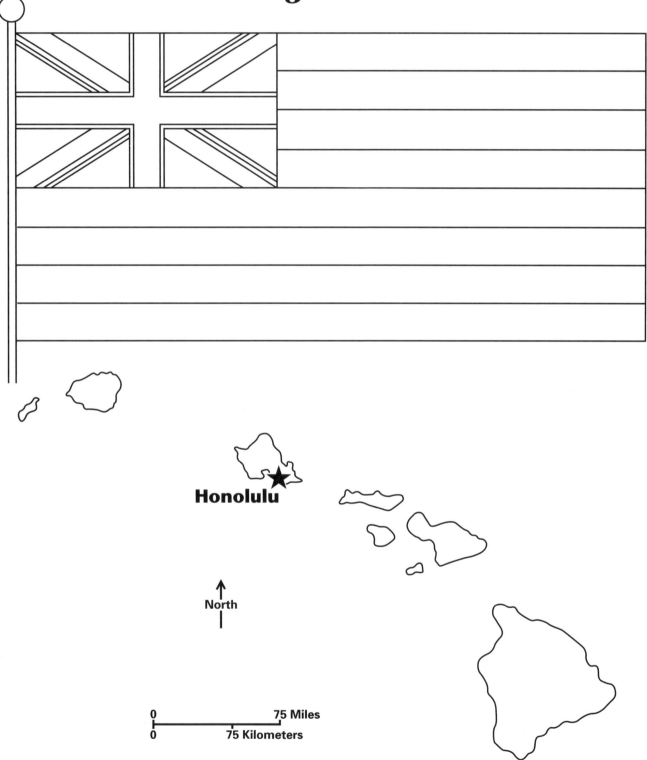

Honolulu

North

0	75 Miles
0	75 Kilometers

Idaho

"Let It Be Perpetual"

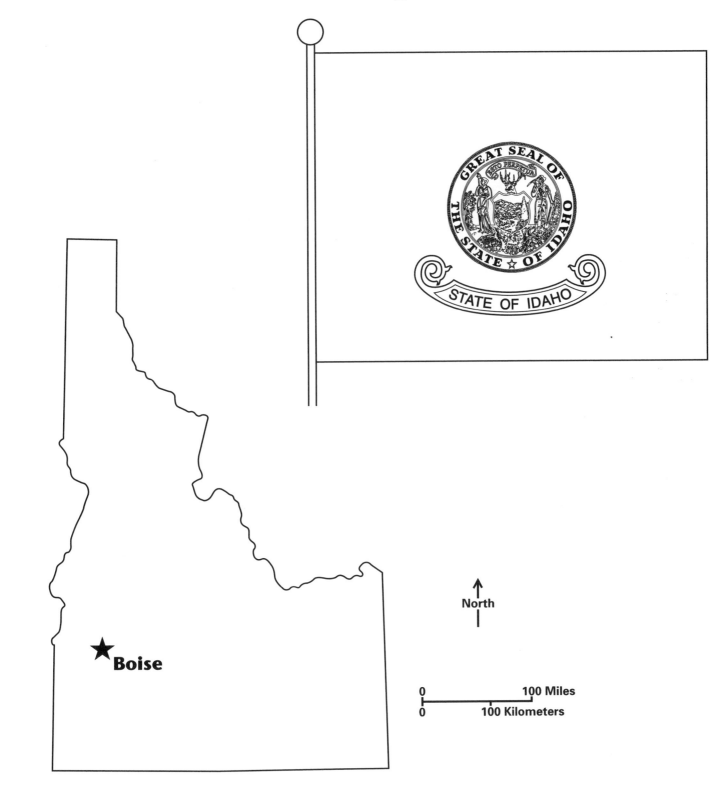

North

0 ___ 100 Miles
0 ___ 100 Kilometers

★ **Boise**

21

Illinois

"State Sovereignty, National Union"

North

Springfield
★

0   75 Miles
0   75 Kilometers

Indiana

"The Crossroads of America"

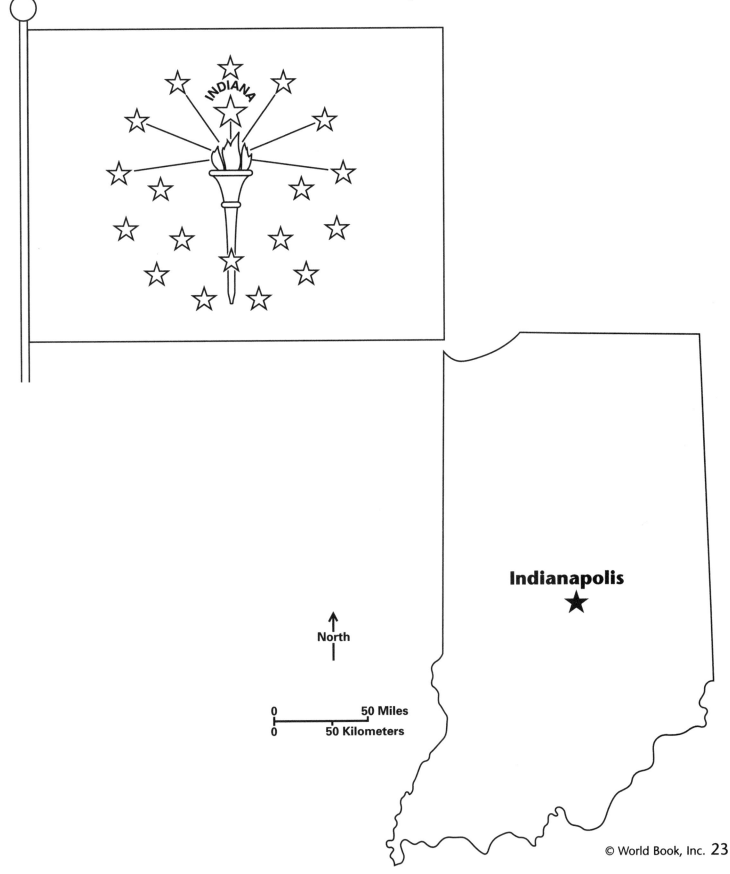

INDIANA

Indianapolis

★

North

0   50 Miles

0   50 Kilometers

Iowa

"Our Liberties We Prize and Our Rights We Will Maintain"

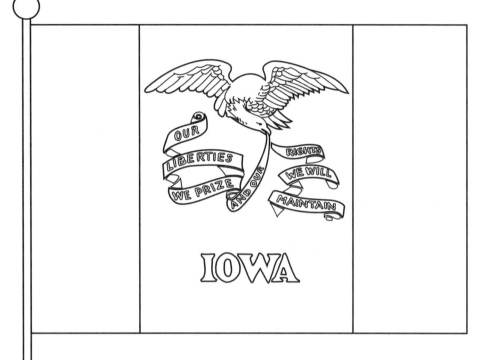

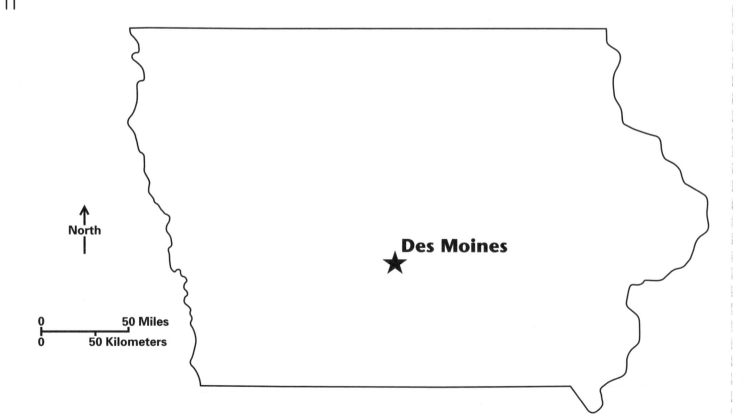

North

Des Moines

0   50 Miles
0   50 Kilometers

Kansas

"To the Stars Through Difficulties"

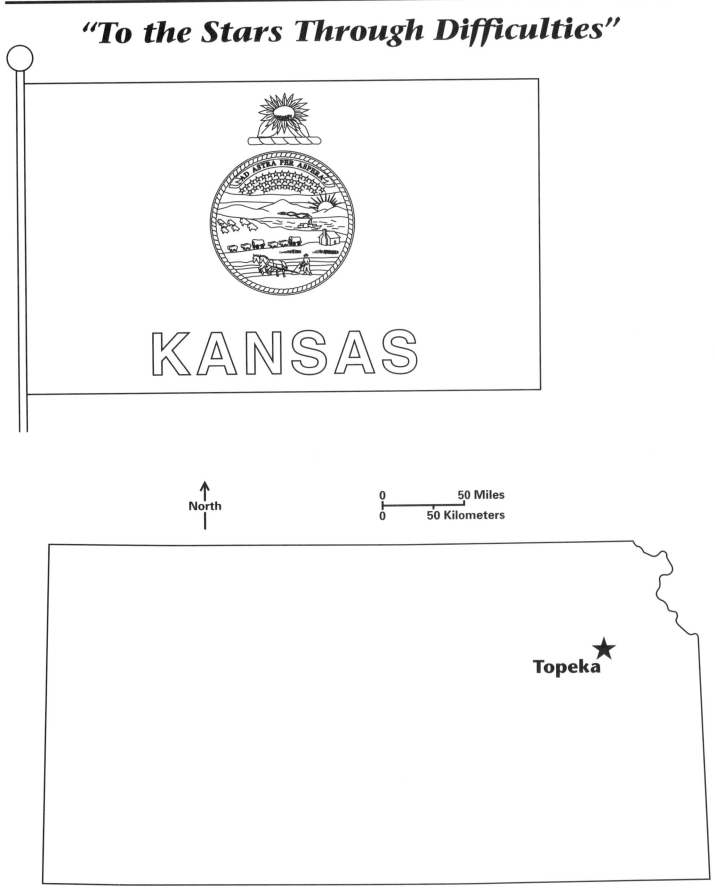

KANSAS

North

| 0 | | 50 Miles |
| 0 | | 50 Kilometers |

Topeka ★

Kentucky

"United We Stand, Divided We Fall"

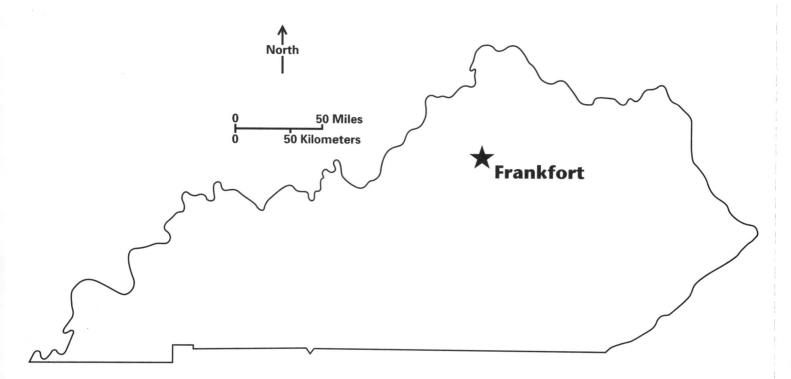

North

0 ——————— 50 Miles
0 ——————— 50 Kilometers

★ Frankfort

Louisiana

"Union, Justice, and Confidence"

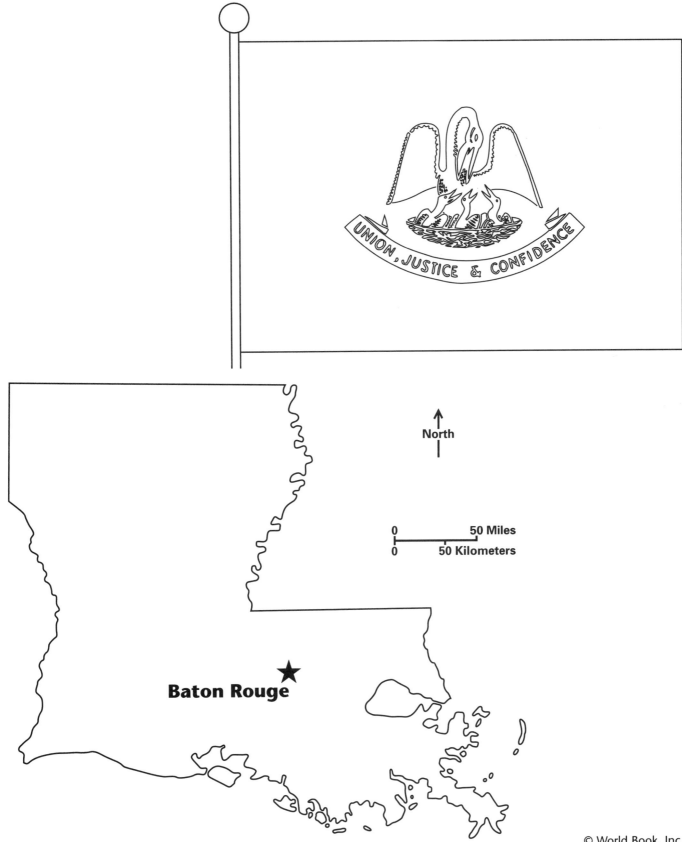

North

0   50 Miles
0   50 Kilometers

Baton Rouge ★

Maine

"I Direct" or "I Guide"

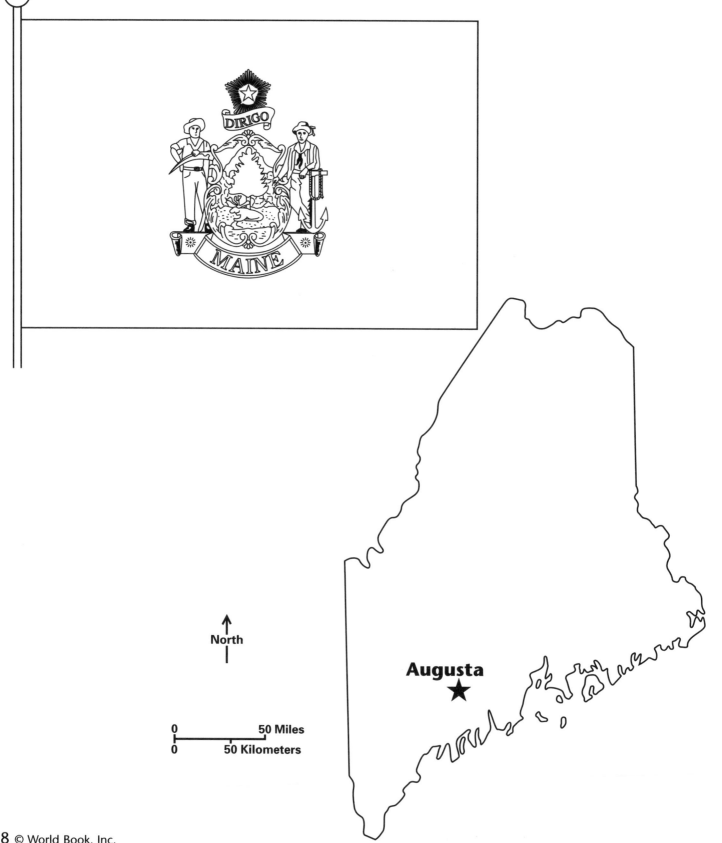

North

0   50 Miles
0   50 Kilometers

Augusta
★

Maryland

"Manly Deeds, Womanly Words"

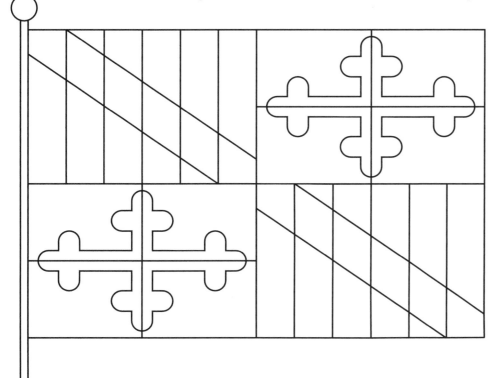

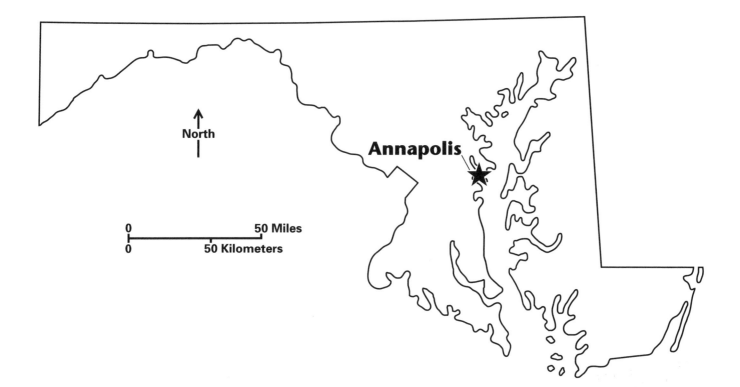

North

Annapolis

0   50 Miles
0   50 Kilometers

Massachusetts

"By the Sword We Seek Peace, but Peace Only Under Liberty"

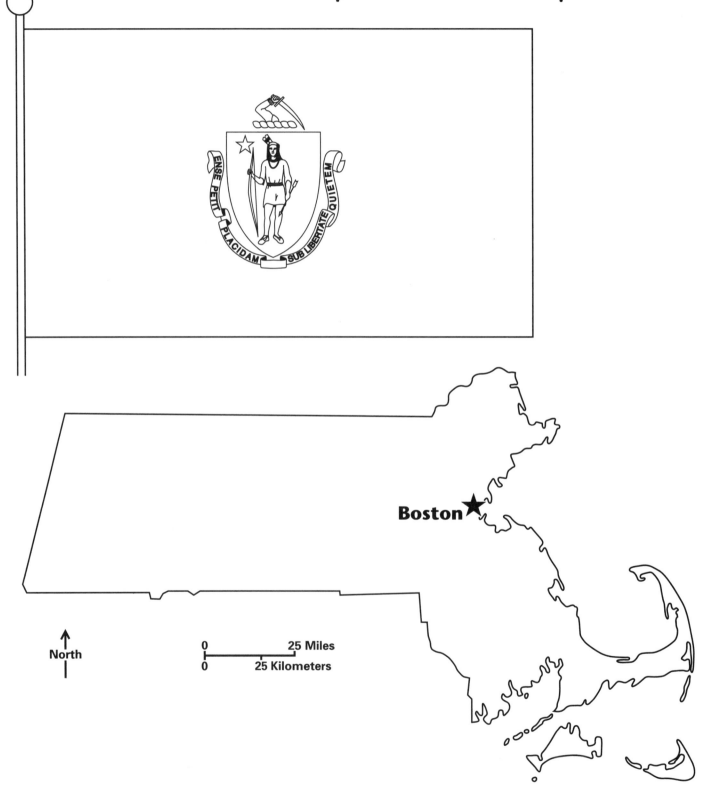

ENSE PETIT PLACIDAM SUB LIBERTATE QUIETEM

Boston

North

0   25 Miles
0   25 Kilometers

Michigan

"If You Seek a Pleasant Peninsula, Look About You"

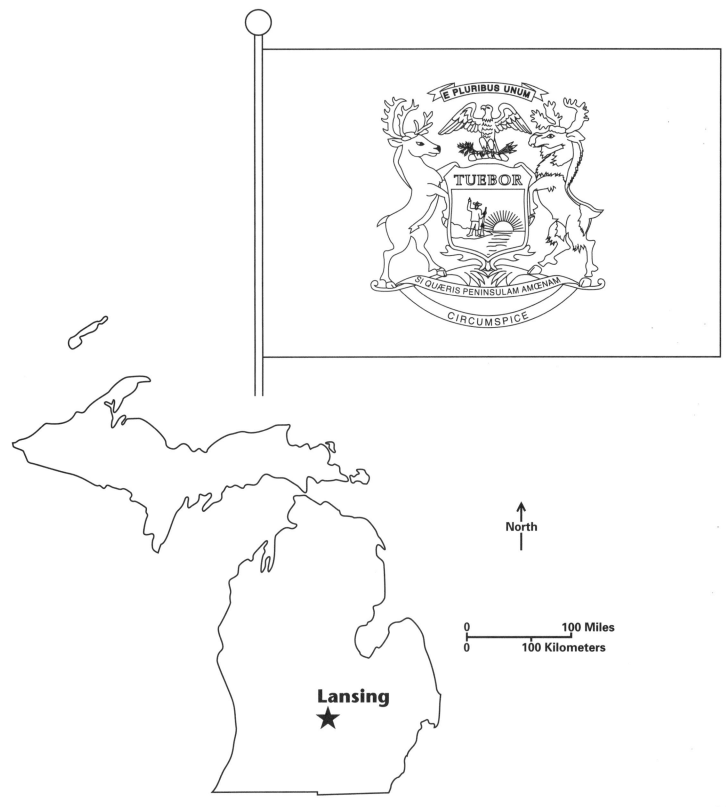

North

| 0 | 100 Miles |
| 0 | 100 Kilometers |

Lansing
★

Minnesota

"The Star of the North"

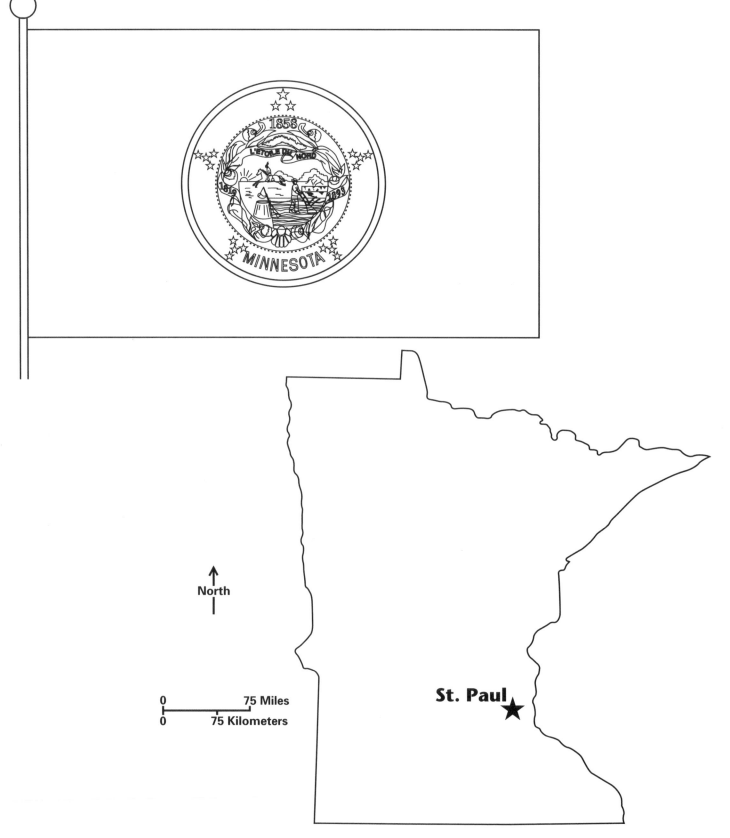

North

0   75 Miles
0   75 Kilometers

St. Paul ★

Mississippi

"By Valor and Arms"

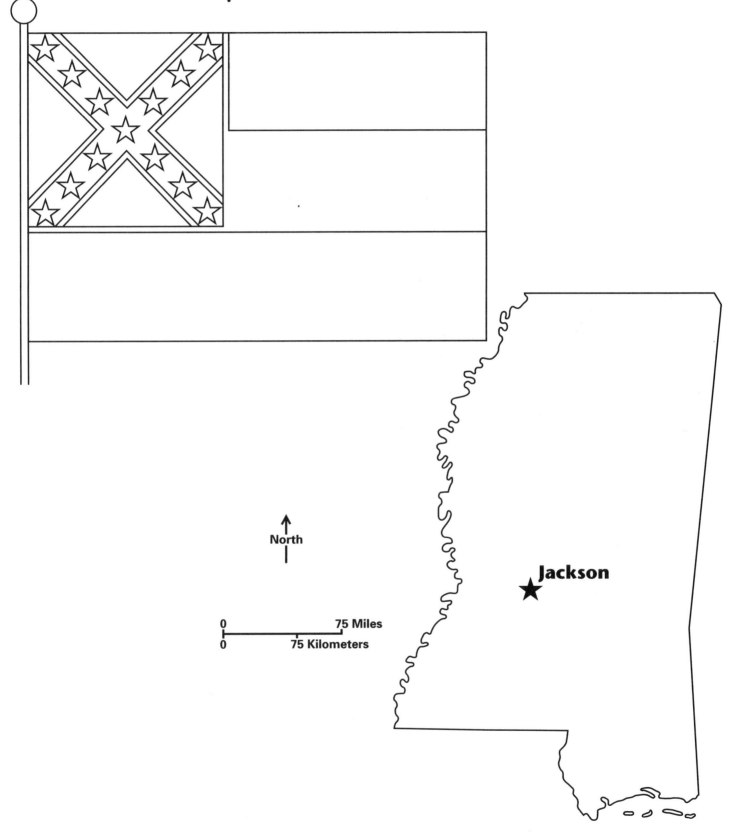

North

Jackson

0   75 Miles
0   75 Kilometers

Missouri

"The Welfare of the People Shall Be the Supreme Law"

North

Jefferson City ★

0   75 Miles

0   75 Kilometers

Montana

"Gold and Silver"

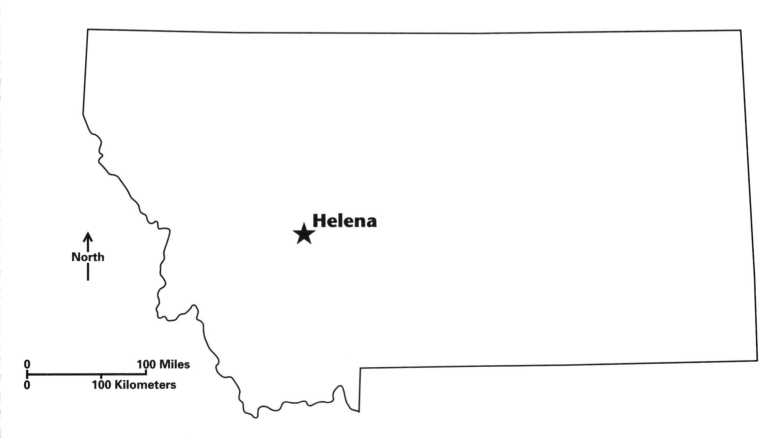

Helena

North

0   100 Miles
0   100 Kilometers

Nebraska

"Equality Before the Law"

North

0   75 Miles
0   75 Kilometers

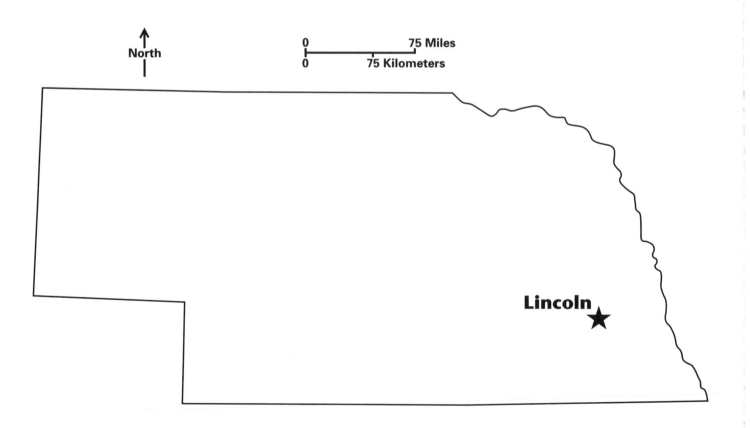

Lincoln ★

Nevada

"All for Our Country"

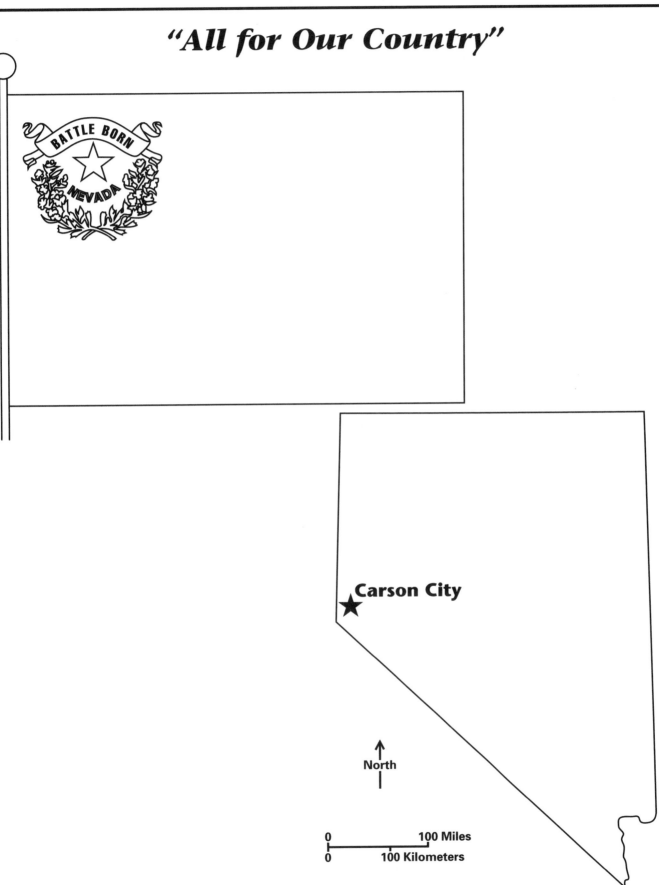

Carson City

North

0   100 Miles
0   100 Kilometers

New Hampshire

"Live Free or Die"

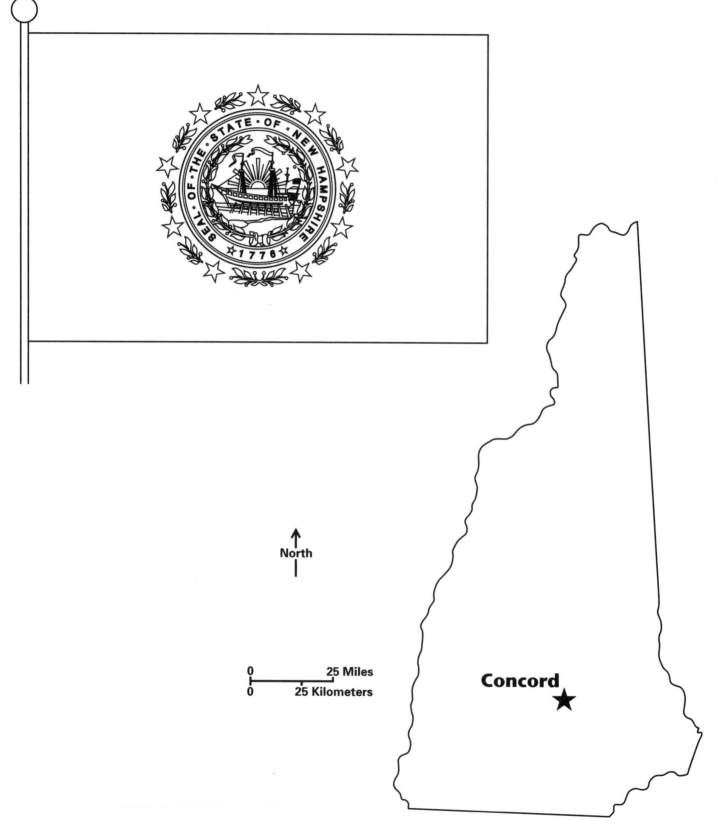

North

0   25 Miles
0   25 Kilometers

Concord ★

New Jersey

"Liberty and Prosperity"

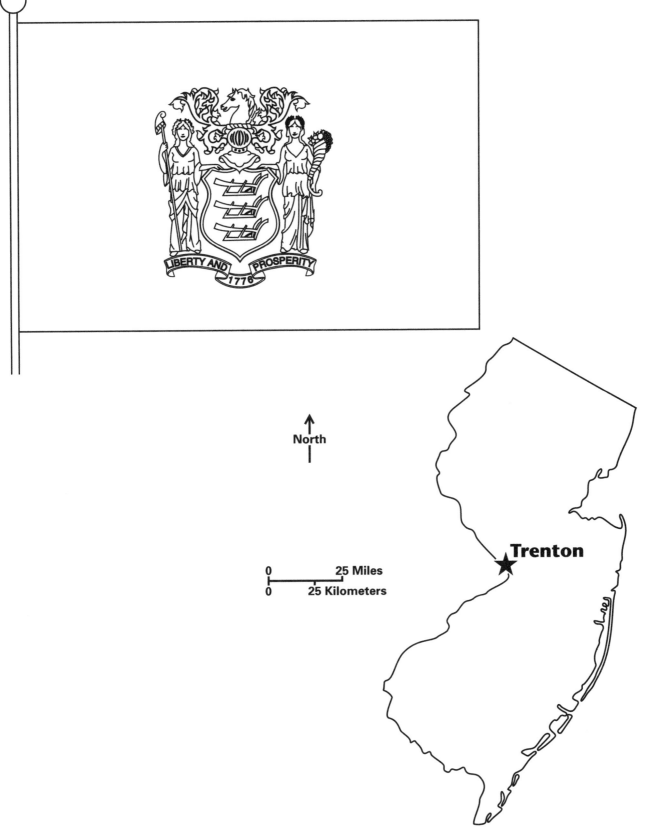

North

0   25 Miles

0   25 Kilometers

★ Trenton

New Mexico

"It Grows as It Goes"

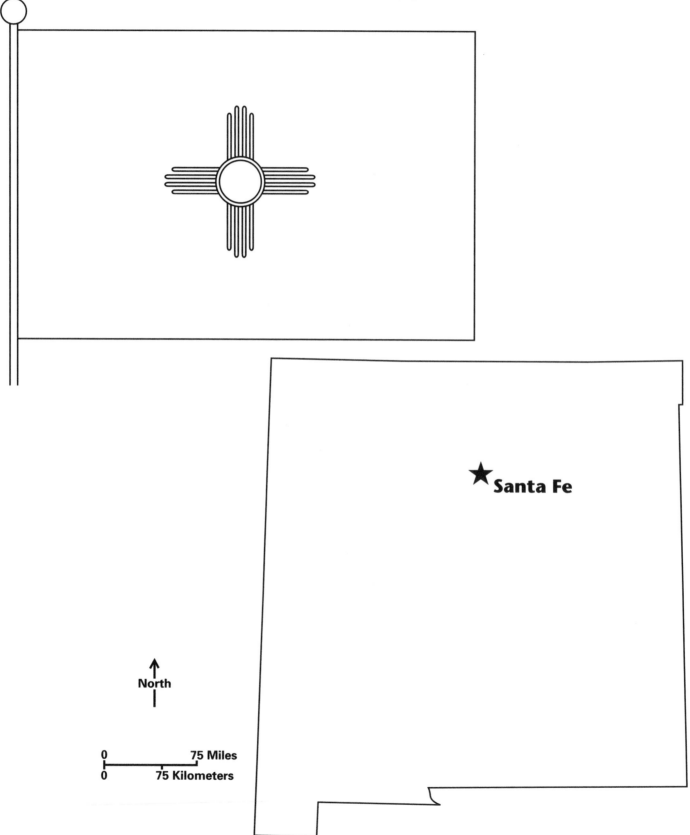

★ Santa Fe

North

0   75 Miles
0   75 Kilometers

New York

"Ever Upward"

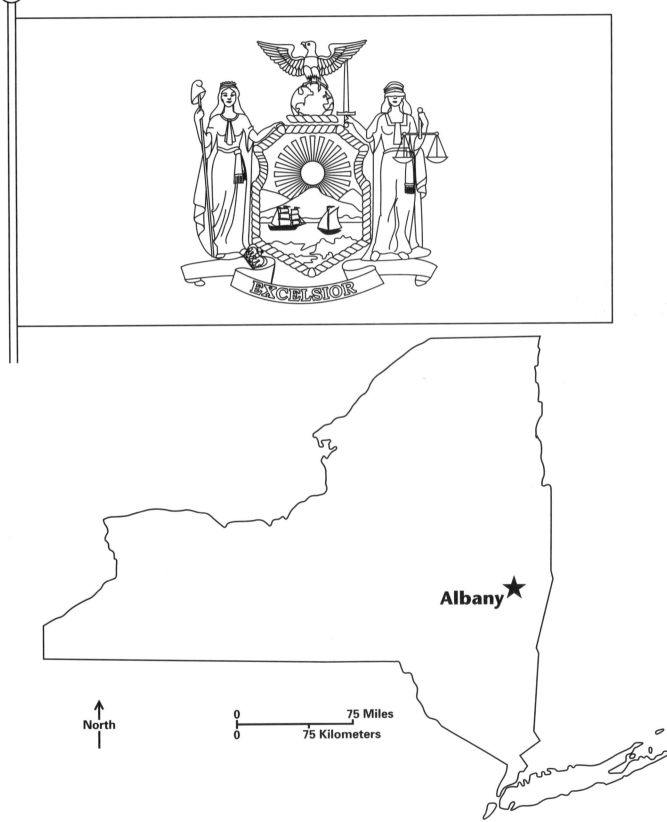

EXCELSIOR

Albany ★

North

0 _____ 75 Miles
0 _____ 75 Kilometers

41

North Carolina

"To Be, Rather Than to Seem"

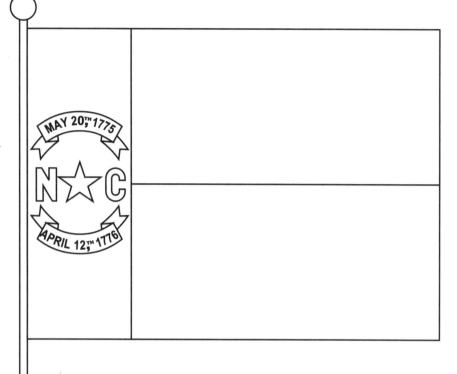

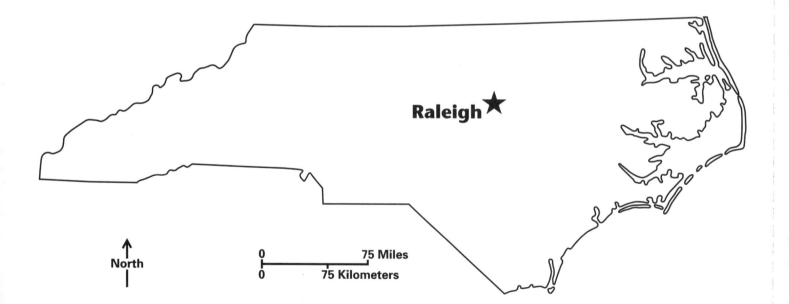

Raleigh

North

0   75 Miles

0   75 Kilometers

North Dakota

"Liberty and Union, Now and Forever, One and Inseparable"

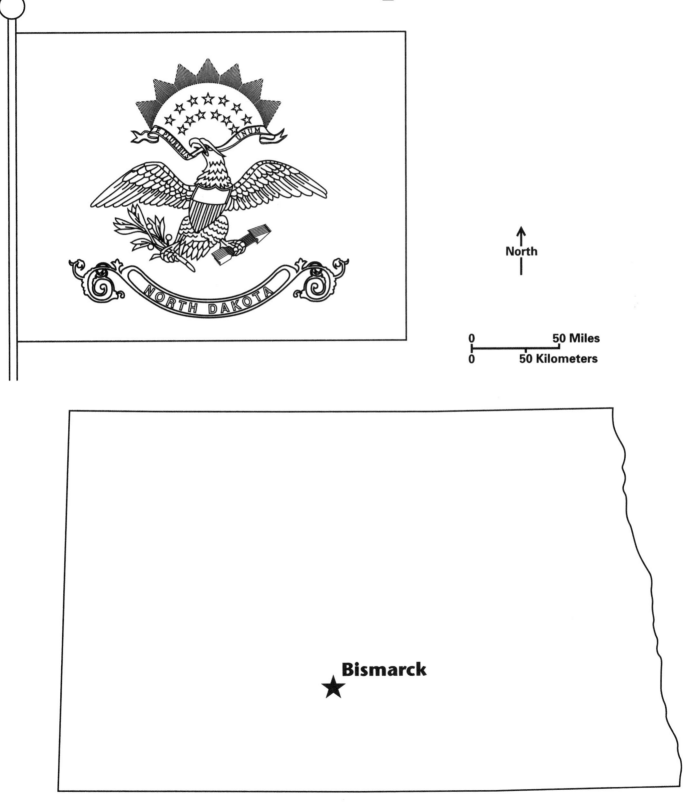

North

| 0 | 50 Miles |
| 0 | 50 Kilometers |

★ **Bismarck**

Ohio

"With God, All Things Are Possible"

North

0   50 Miles
0   50 Kilometers

★ Columbus

Oklahoma

"Labor Conquers All Things"

OKLAHOMA

North

Oklahoma City

| 0 | 75 Miles |
| 0 | 75 Kilometers |

45

Oregon

"She Flies with Her Own Wings"

© World Book, Inc.

Pennsylvania

"Virtue, Liberty, and Independence"

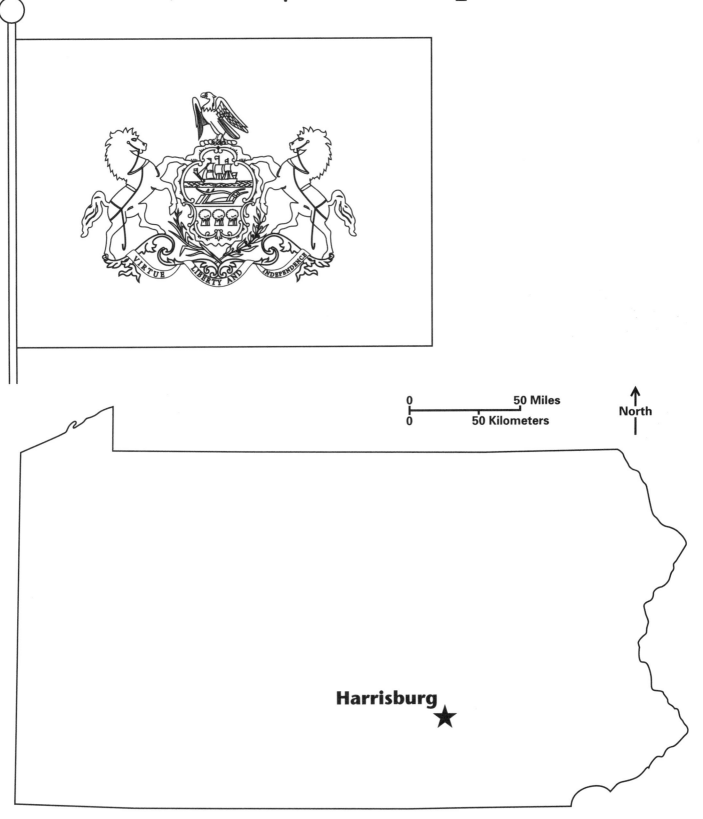

0   **50 Miles**

0   **50 Kilometers**

North

Harrisburg ★

47

Rhode Island

"Hope"

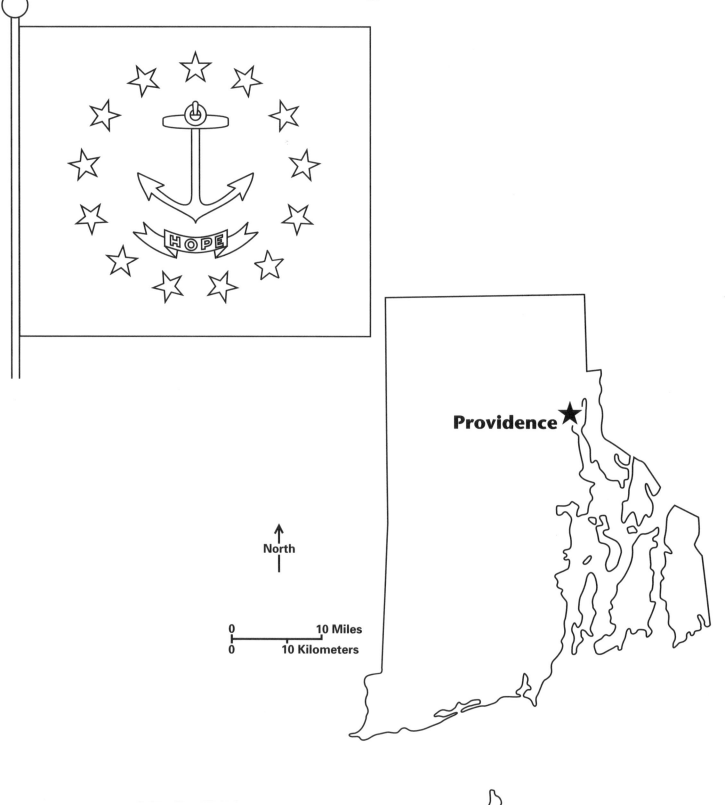

North

| 0 | 10 Miles |
| 0 | 10 Kilometers |

Providence ★

South Carolina

"Prepared in Mind and Resources" and "While I Breathe, I Hope"

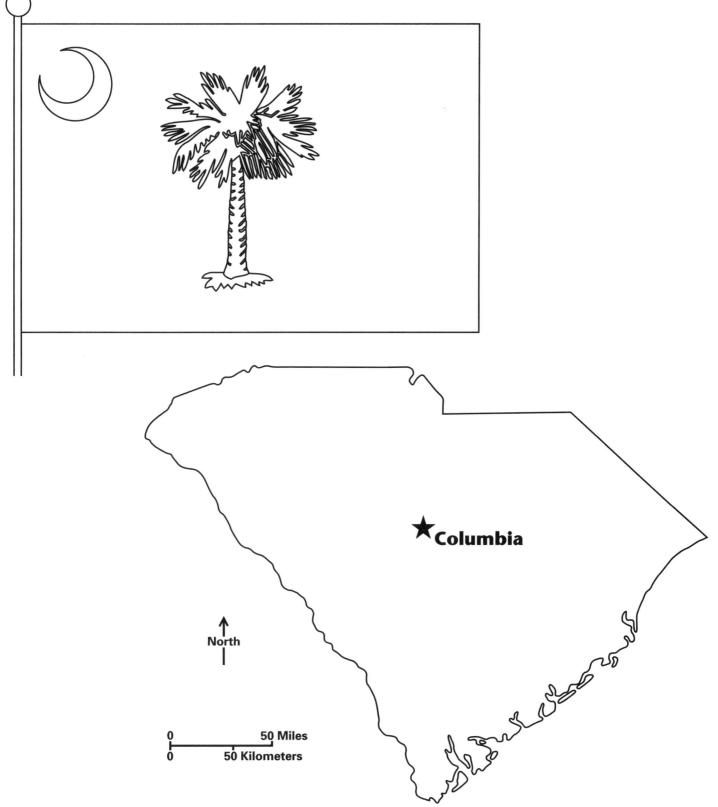

★ Columbia

↑
North

0   50 Miles
0   50 Kilometers

South Dakota

"Under God the People Rule"

North

0 — 50 Miles
0 — 50 Kilometers

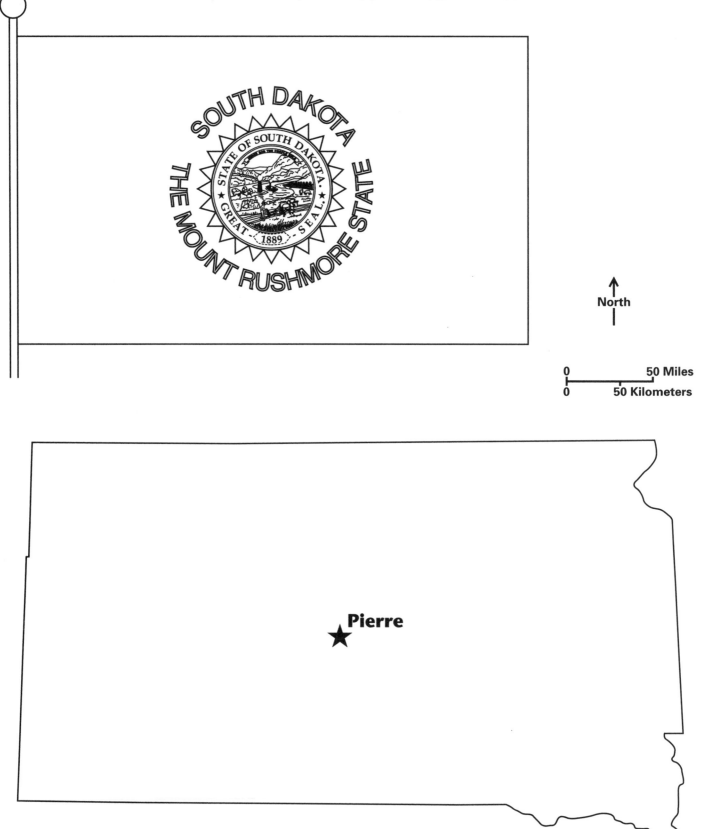

★ Pierre

Tennessee

"Agriculture and Commerce"

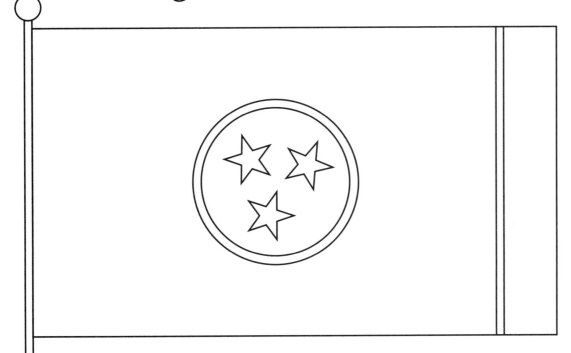

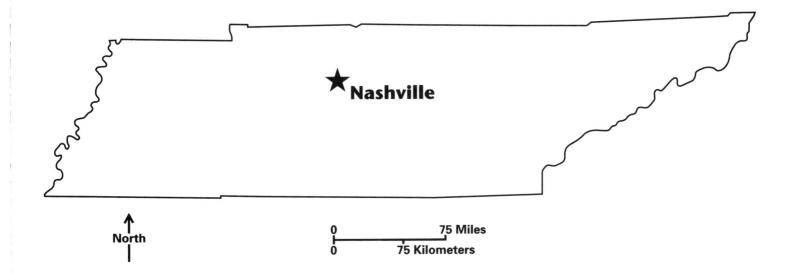

★ **Nashville**

North

| 0 | 75 Miles |
| 0 | 75 Kilometers |

Texas

"Friendship"

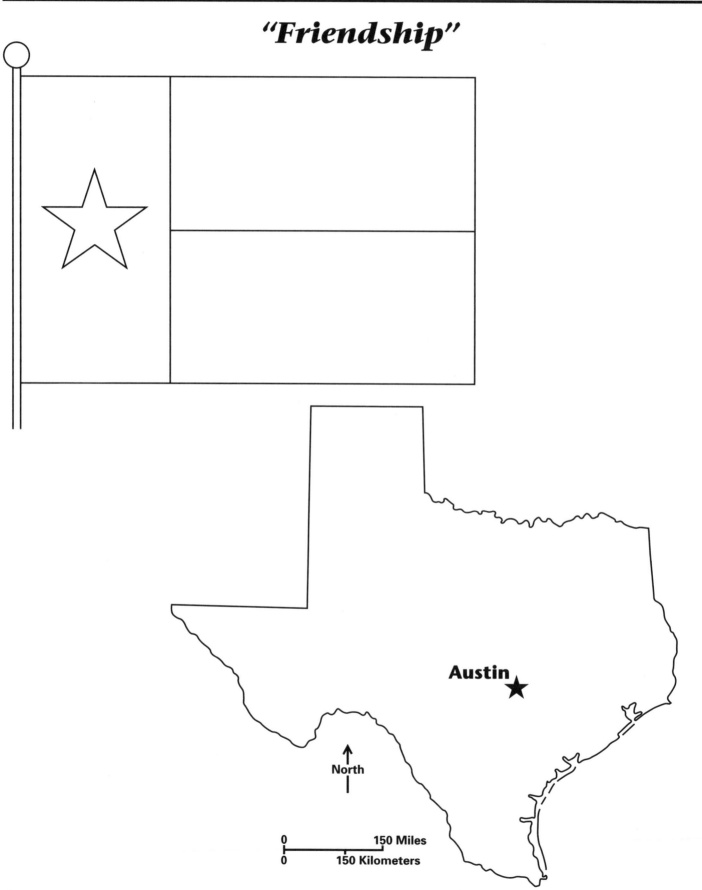

Austin ★

North

| 0 | | 150 Miles |
| 0 | | 150 Kilometers |

Utah

"Industry"

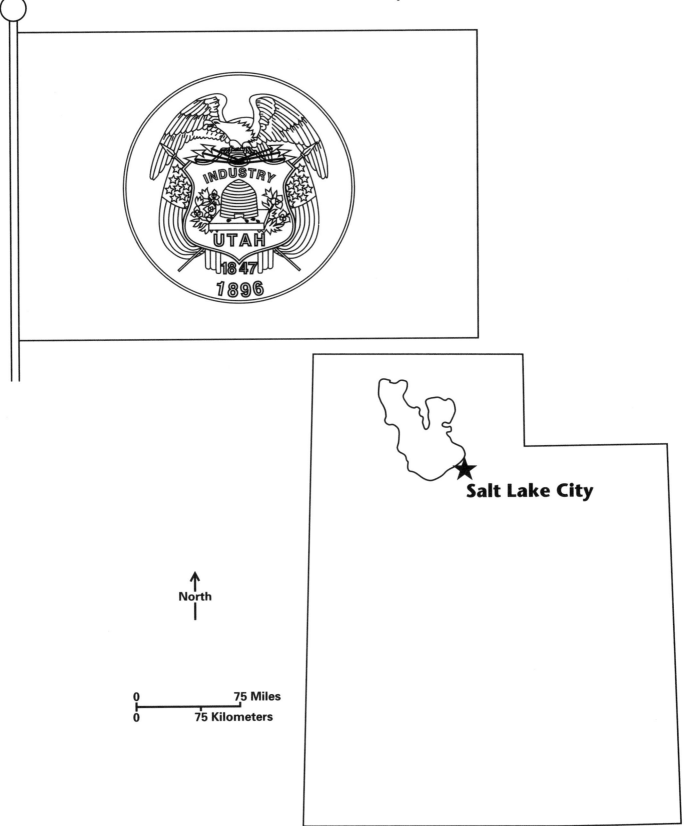

INDUSTRY

UTAH

1847
1896

Salt Lake City

North

0   75 Miles
0   75 Kilometers

Vermont

"Freedom and Unity"

North

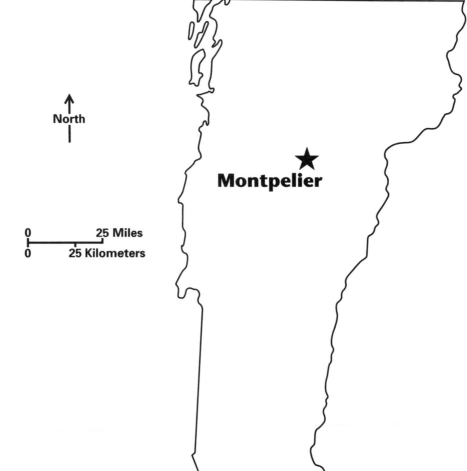

★
Montpelier

0   25 Miles
0   25 Kilometers

Virginia

"Thus Always to Tyrants"

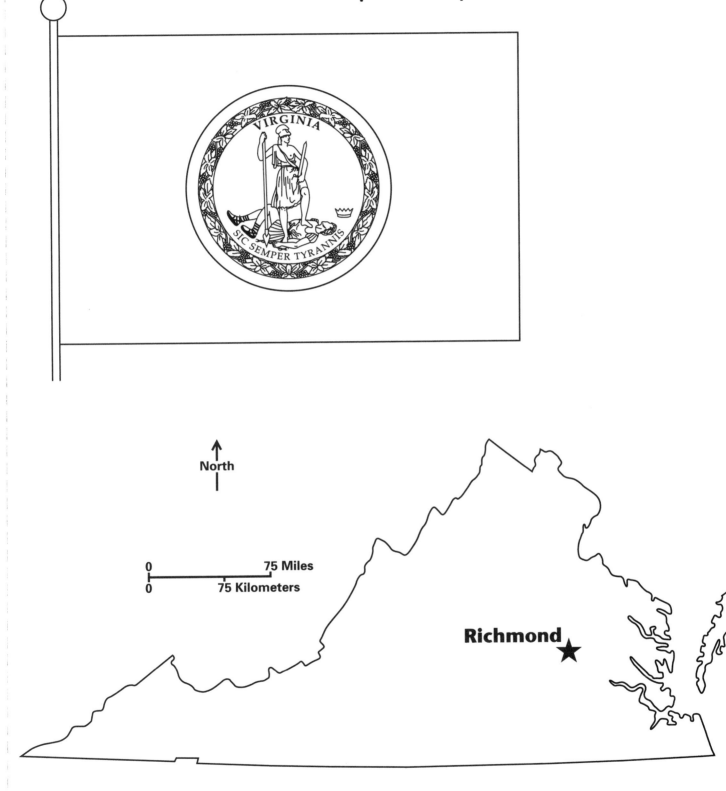

North

0   75 Miles

0   75 Kilometers

Richmond ★

Washington

"Bye and Bye"

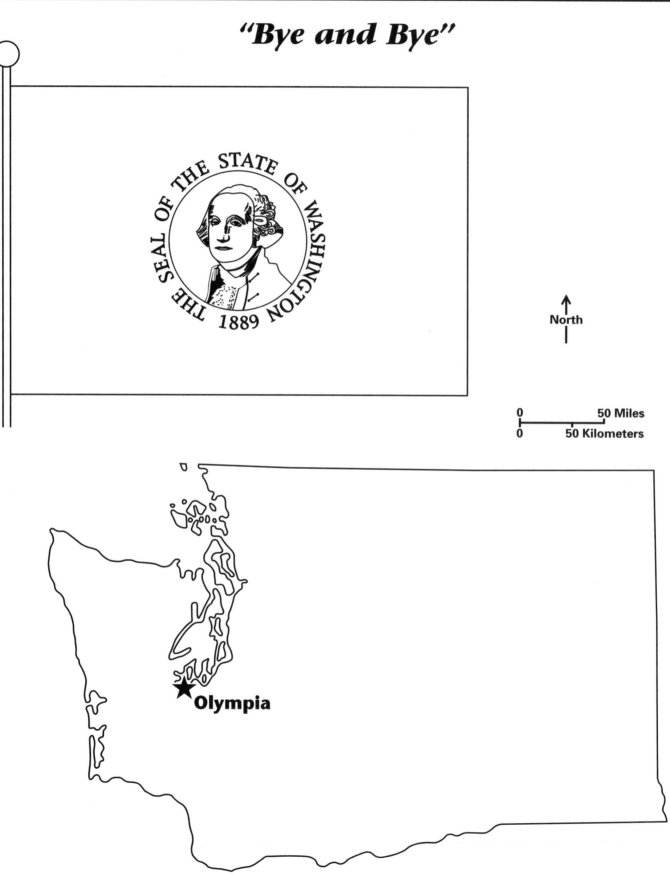

THE SEAL OF THE STATE OF WASHINGTON 1889

North

0   50 Miles
0   50 Kilometers

★ Olympia

West Virginia

"Mountaineers Are Always Free"

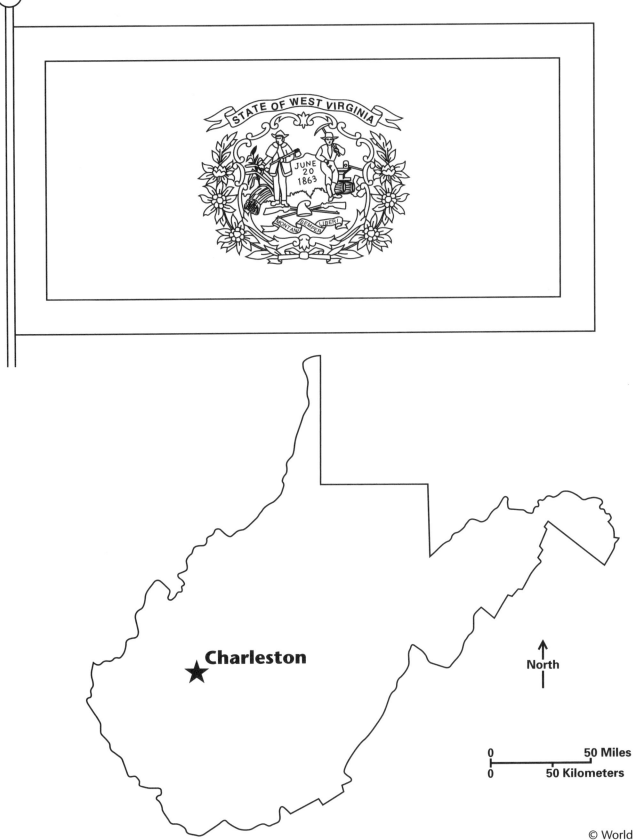

STATE OF WEST VIRGINIA

JUNE 20 1863

MONTANI SEMPER LIBERI

★ **Charleston**

North

| 0 | 50 Miles |
| 0 | 50 Kilometers |

Wisconsin

"Forward"

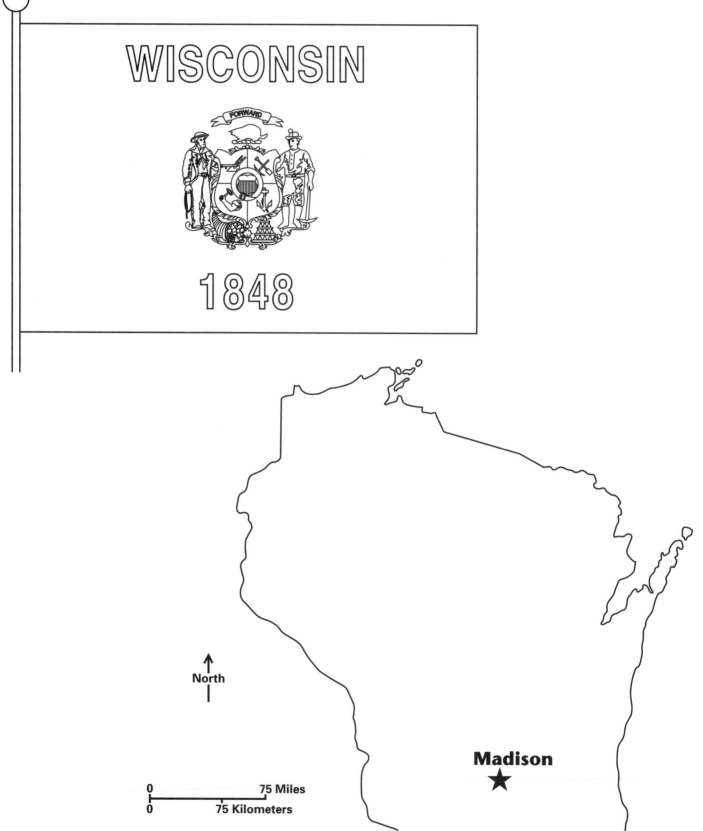

WISCONSIN

FORWARD

1848

North

Madison ★

0   75 Miles
0   75 Kilometers

Wyoming

"Equal Rights"

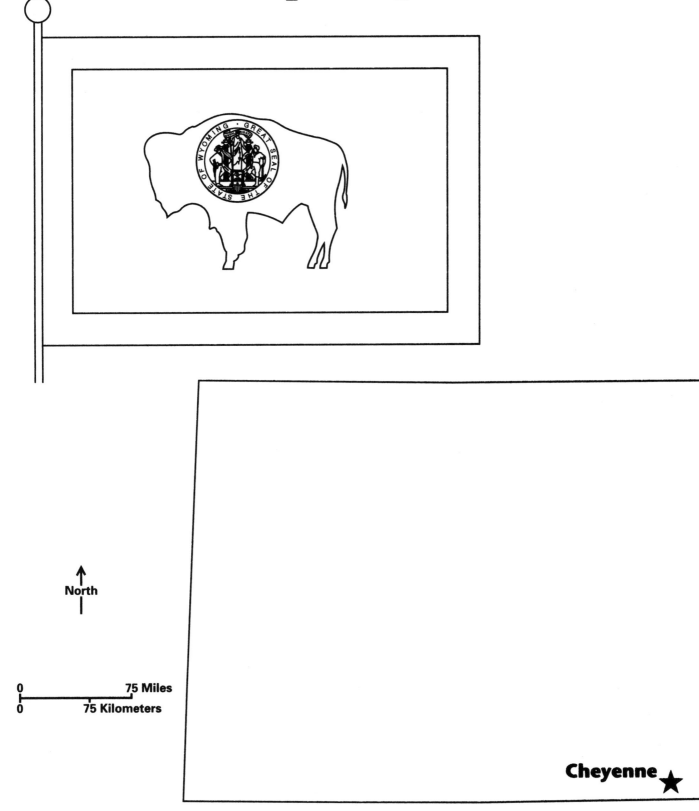

North

0   75 Miles
0   75 Kilometers

Cheyenne ★

Word Search

States East of the Mississippi River

Hidden in the letters below are the names of all the U.S. states east of the Mississippi River. Words may be hidden horizontally, vertically, or diagonally and may be forward or backward. One state is circled already to get you started. When you find the name of a state in the puzzle, circle it and cross it off the list.

```
K E A L S E R N U O H N E W J E R S E Y F P E
D N A L S I E D O H R T R E B N L E S A S C V
P I E E A X L I R R S W I S C O N S I N P C X
U A R W Z B W O N G A R S T P O N O O G H O R
B M A R Y L A N D A R H J V O E V U N M P P E
S I I P N O J M T D E S S I E A P T I S I O B
A S N C Y O R S A I P O A R B N T H L D R V E
P S I Y H E R K D R I N U G H O E C L A E P R
R I G N O I L E N O I A P I S M N A I R E E A
W S R M Z E G W F L M I E N Q U K R M C E N W
O S I W V S A A O F A M L I W O N O R I A N A
C I V B P H W R N T F I O A X E N L K I T S L
F P M A S S A C H U S E T T S T N I D U B Y E
M P R R E C D F I H R B Y K C U T N E K O L D
E I S D H J Y E V J O G E O R G I A A T V V M
M R T T E N N E S S E E N H R J B S K E I A O
E E R T N E W H A M P S H I R E K F E N J N O
M O R T T U C I T C E N N O C V N M R E E I P
N K L R D O J Y F R T J K S Y K M E R L I A O
```

Alabama	Illinois	Massachusetts	New York	South Carolina
Connecticut	Indiana	Michigan	North Carolina	Tennessee
Delaware	Kentucky	Mississippi	Ohio	~~Vermont~~
Florida	Maine	New Hampshire	Pennsylvania	Virginia
Georgia	Maryland	New Jersey	Rhode Island	West Virginia
				Wisconsin

Word Search

States West of the Mississippi River

Hidden in the letters below are the names of all the U.S. states west of the Mississippi River. Words may be hidden horizontally, vertically, or diagonally and may be forward or backward. One state is circled already to get you started. When you find the name of a state in the puzzle, circle it and cross it off the list.

```
A N W P S S E G I N B R E D V K L E I F O
R O D A R O L O C K C O N R M O E A D R P
S T R E S E C L W R E A I M C S P W B I A
A B X H M H E B P I S R M O H A K B M S A
R G T C A L I F O R N I A A Y S A X E T N
L L F W W K A N A E O Z R J E N H I O W A
G O A R I U N O G E R O N J O A M S D N I
N I T A B H E W A T N N E E L K E V A P S
I D O V Q U V G N O A O N E N T I C E I
M A K S A L A P B K E N W R N R F H A T U
O H A O U S D A D V O W A I Y A U X G N O
Y O D A C M A N A T N O M B A N E A K A L
W M H K S O L N E T I T L E B I O J M R V
J O T C O I W E D B S P I L X R T O E K R
E F U D P A S T Y U R E W D H I H I S A E
W R O N H G C T A I M A I U O A C S J N S
M I S S O U R I E M R Z S O L H I O N S Z
U P E F O C G L U A L U E K P U H U F A I
I K Y E N O R T H D A K O T A N E Q Y S A
```

Alaska	Hawaii	Minnesota	New Mexico	Texas
Arizona	Idaho	Missouri	North Dakota	Utah
Arkansas	Iowa	Montana	Oklahoma	Washington
California	Kansas	~~Nebraska~~	Oregon	Wyoming
Colorado	Louisiana	Nevada	South Dakota	

500 Miles

500 Kilometers

North

Canada

"From Sea to Sea"

Ottawa

63

Canada Facts and Symbols

The flag of Canada features a red, 11-pointed maple leaf, a national symbol of the country. It became Canada's official flag in 1965.

The beaver, found in the northern part of the world, is also a national symbol of Canada.

The Canadian coat of arms includes three red maple leaves below the royal arms of England, Scotland, Ireland, and France.

Canada is the second largest country in the world, but the 36th in population.

Canada consists of 10 provinces and 3 territories. The country's capital is the city of Ottawa in the province of Ontario.

65

Province/Territory Facts

Provinces	Area in sq. mi.	Area in sq. km	Date became province
Alberta	255,287	661,190	1905
British Columbia	365,900	947,800	1871
Manitoba	250,947	649,950	1870
New Brunswick	28,355	73,440	1867
Newfoundland	156,649	405,720	1949
Nova Scotia	21,423	55,490	1867
Ontario	412,581	1,068,580	1867
Prince Edward Island	2,185	5,660	1873
Quebec	594,860	1,540,680	1867
Saskatchewan	251,866	652,330	1905

Territories	Area in sq. mi.	Area in sq. km	Date became territory
Northwest Territories	501,570	1,299,070	1870
Nunavut	770,000	1,900,000	1999
Yukon Territory	186,661	483,450	1898

Alberta

"Strong and Free"

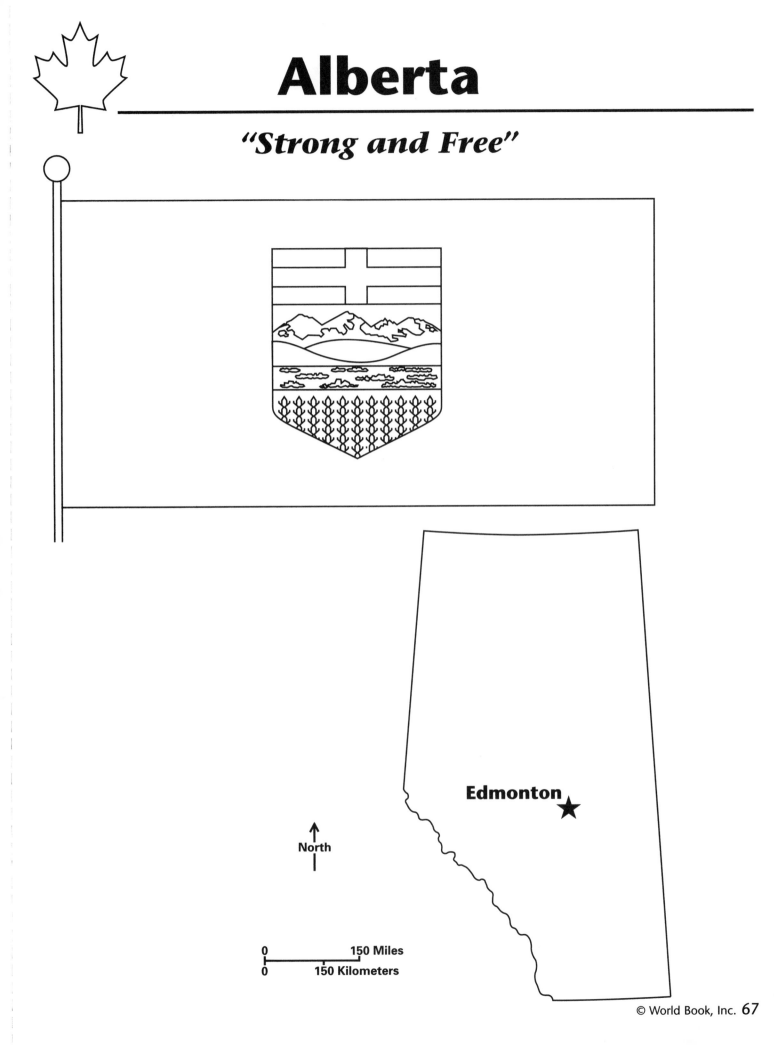

North

Edmonton ★

| 0 | 150 Miles |
| 0 | 150 Kilometers |

67

British Columbia

"Splendor Without Diminishment"

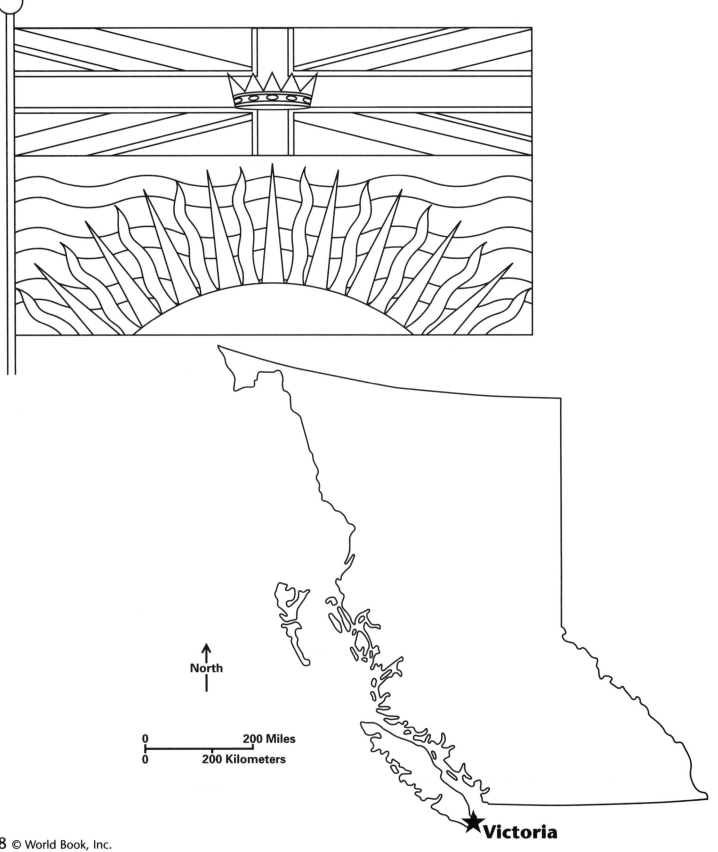

North

0   200 Miles
0   200 Kilometers

★Victoria

Manitoba

(no motto)

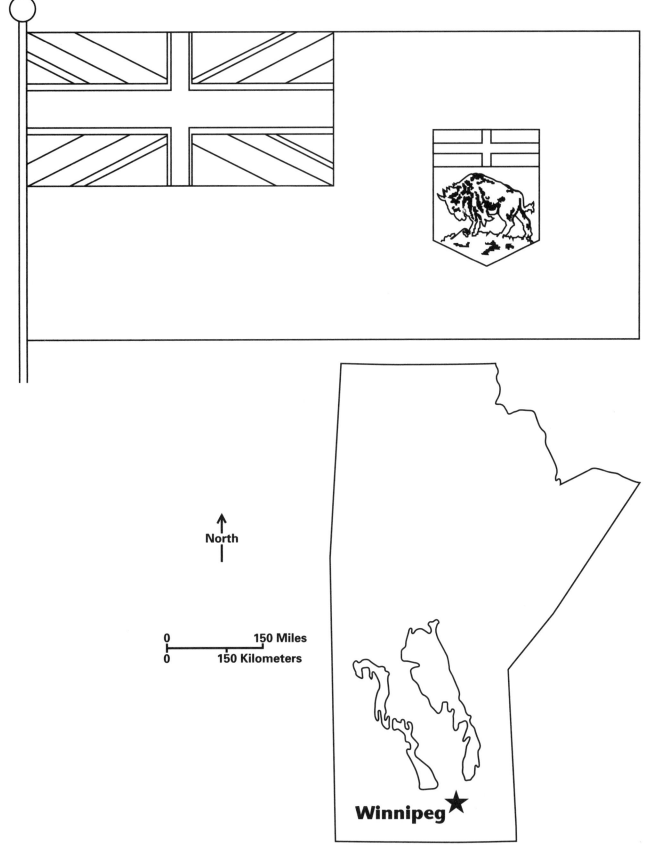

North

0 — 150 Miles
0 — 150 Kilometers

Winnipeg ★

New Brunswick

"Hope Restored"

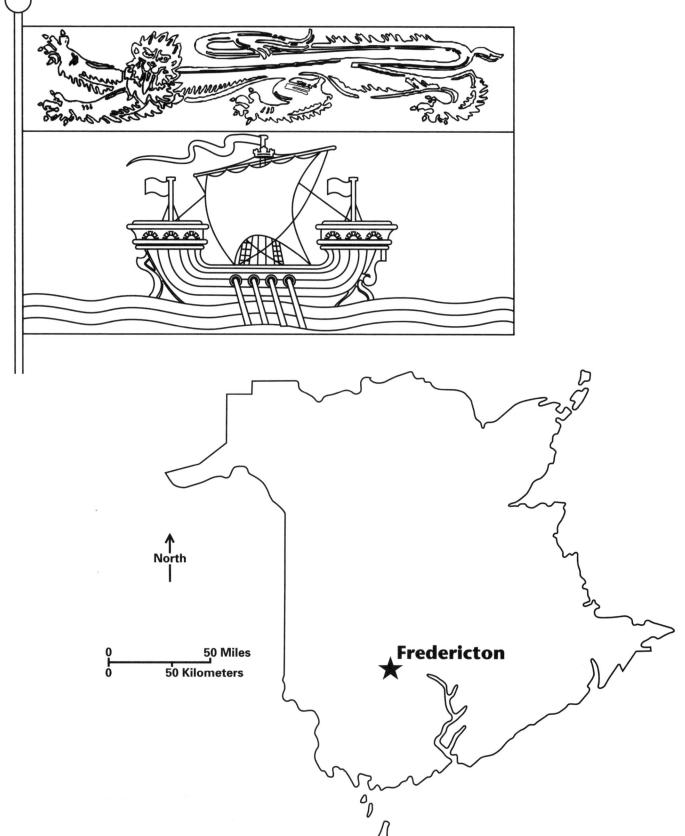

North

0   50 Miles
0   50 Kilometers

★ **Fredericton**

Newfoundland

"Seek Ye First the Kingdom of God"

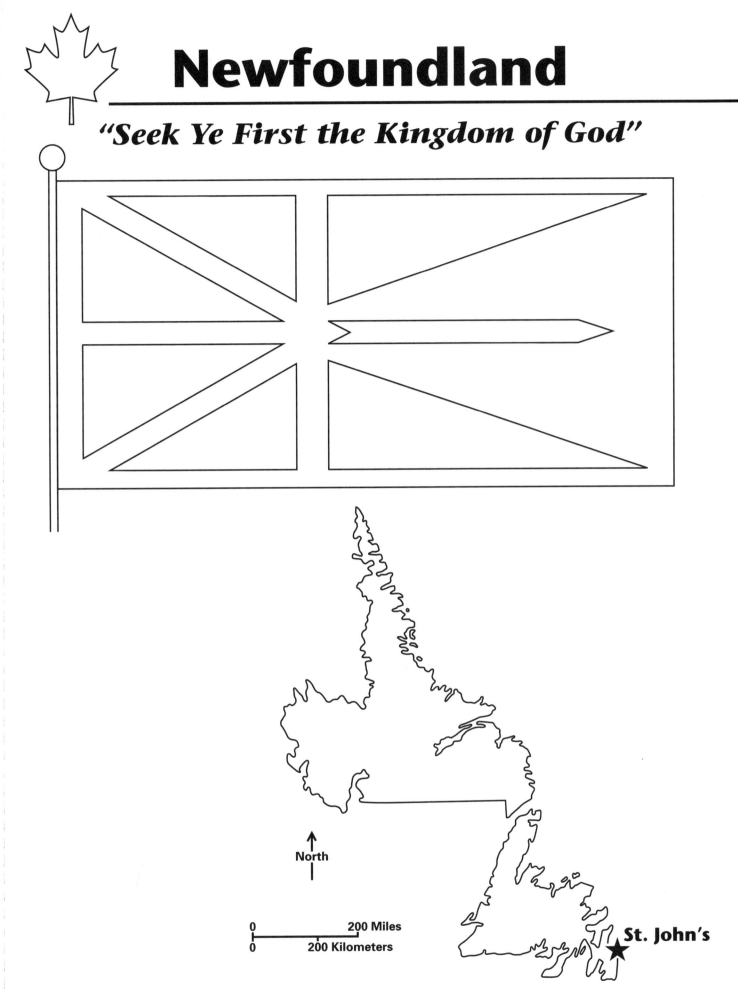

North

| 0 | 200 Miles |
| 0 | 200 Kilometers |

St. John's

71

Northwest Territories

(no motto)

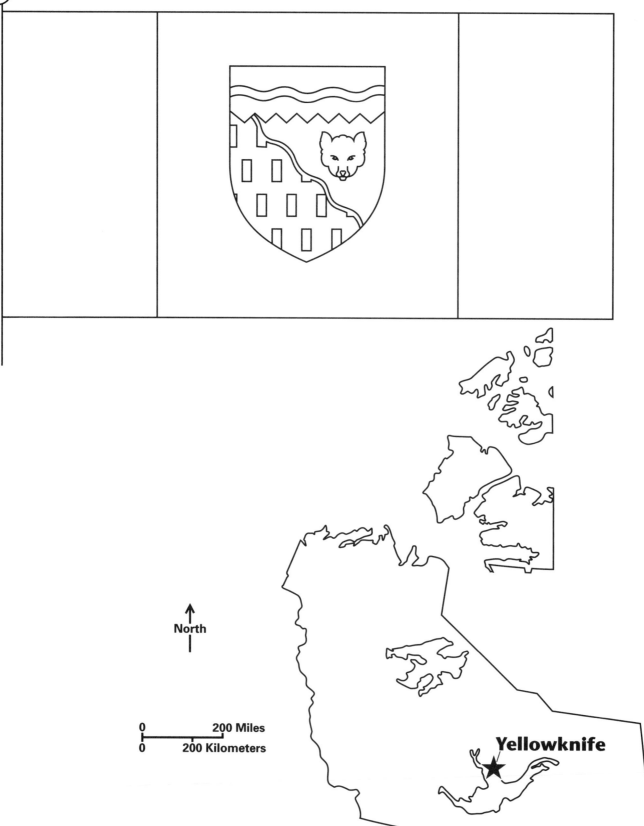

North

0   200 Miles
0   200 Kilometers

Yellowknife

© World Book, Inc.

Nova Scotia

"One Defends and the Other Conquers"

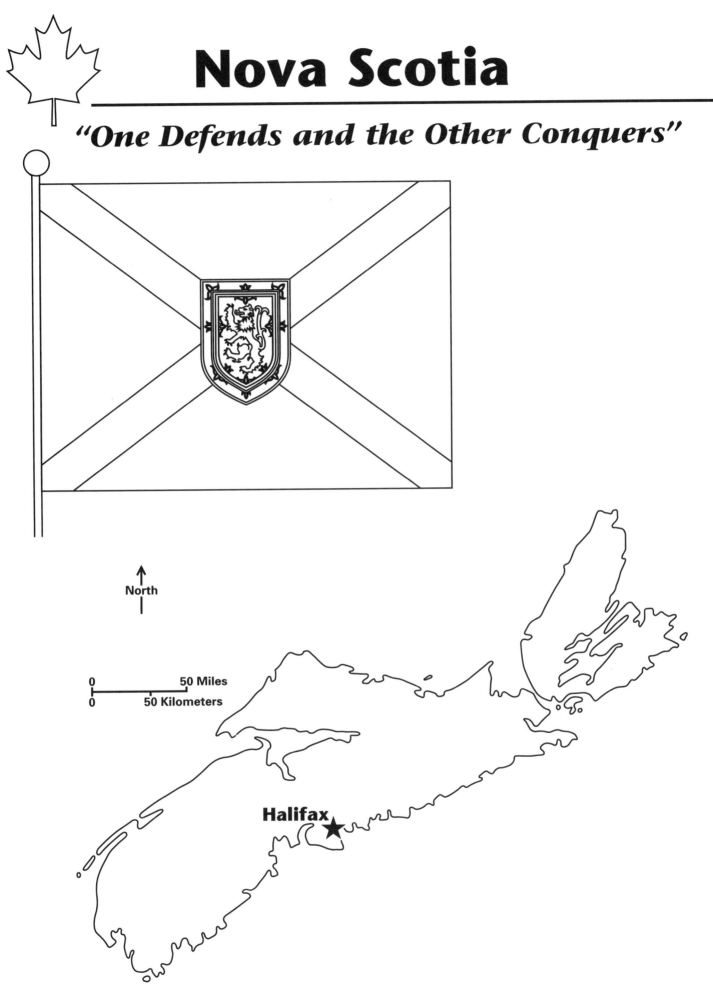

North

0   50 Miles
0   50 Kilometers

Halifax

Nunavut

(no motto)

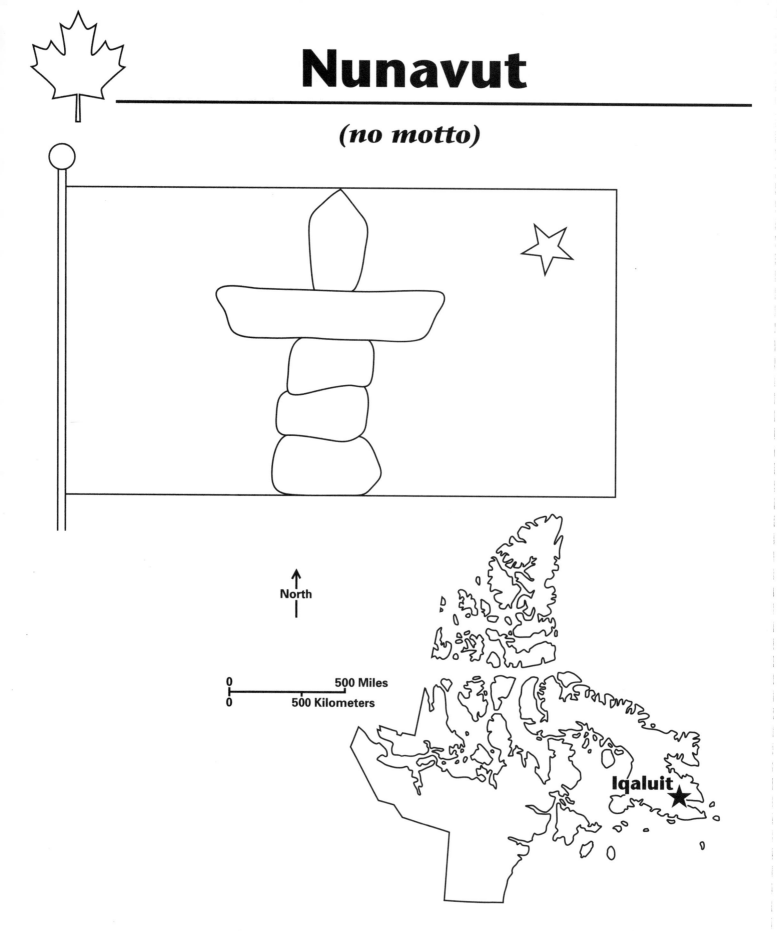

North

| 0 | | | 500 Miles |
| 0 | | | 500 Kilometers |

Iqaluit ★

Ontario

"Loyal She Began, Loyal She Remains"

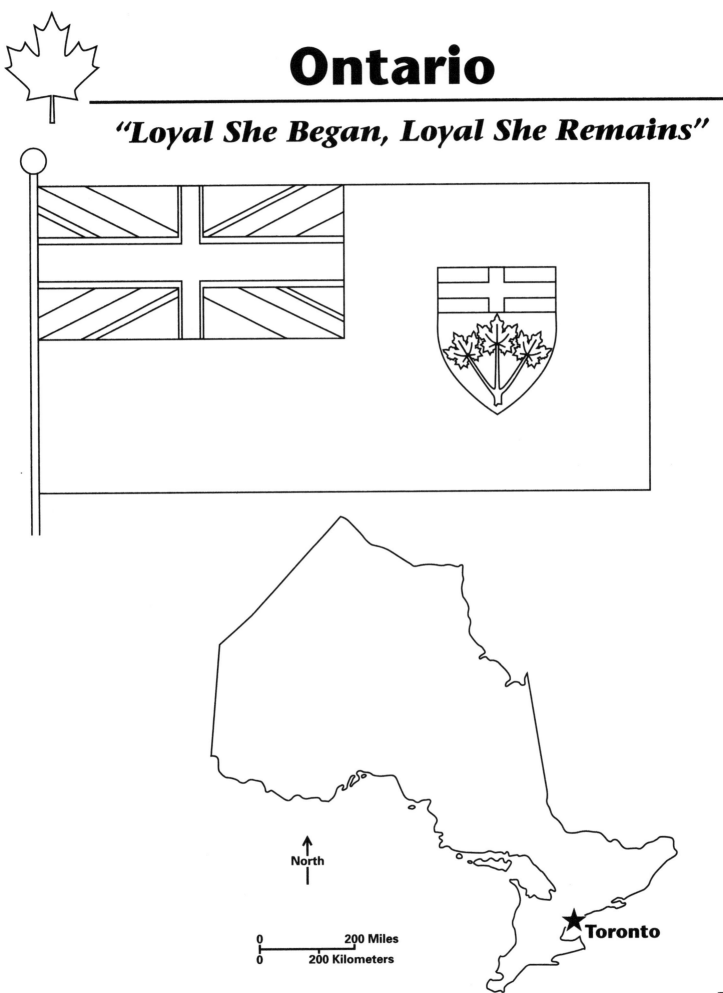

North

0   200 Miles
0   200 Kilometers

★ Toronto

Prince Edward Island

"The Small Under the Protection of the Great"

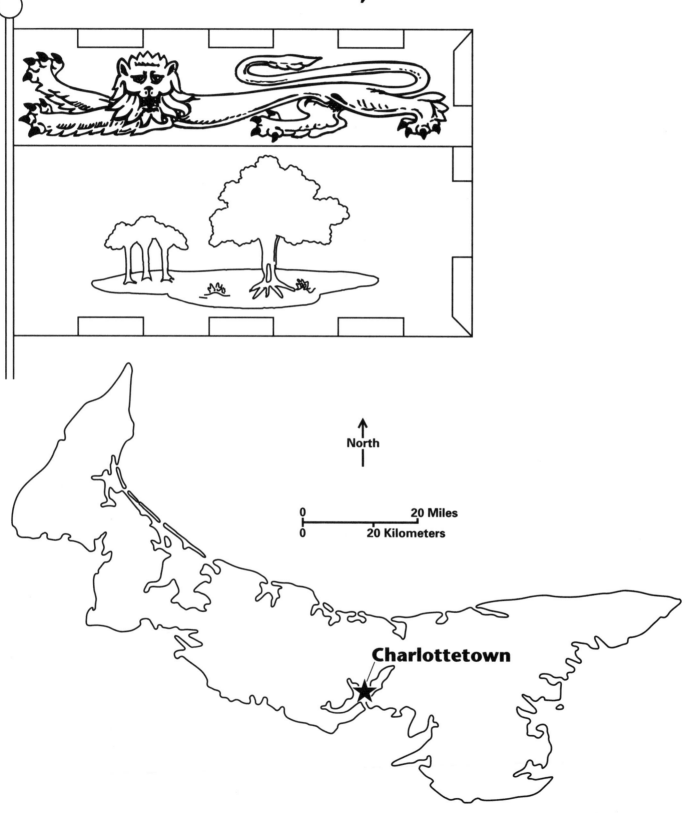

North

0   20 Miles
0   20 Kilometers

★ Charlottetown

Quebec

"I Remember"

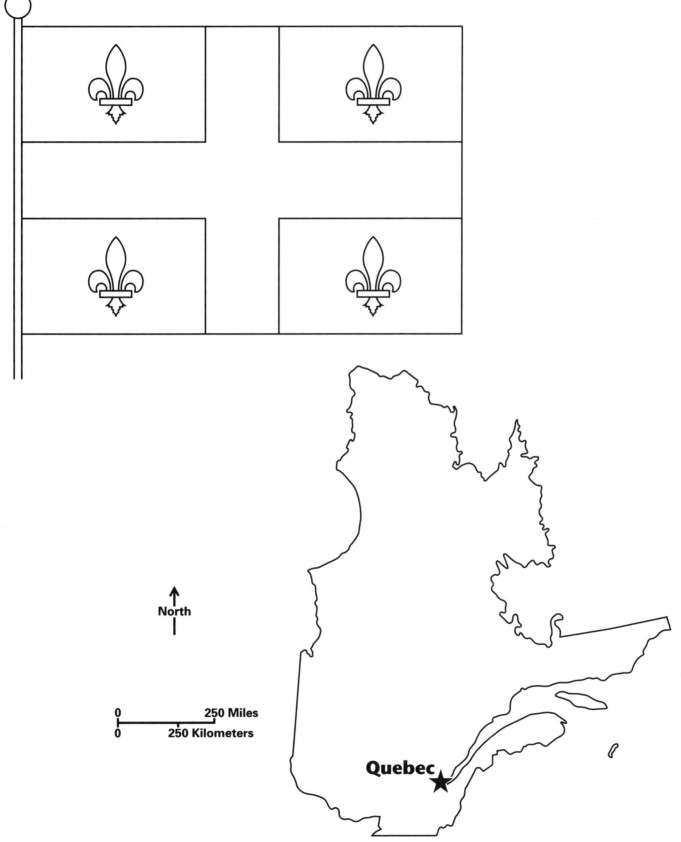

North

| 0 | | 250 Miles |
| 0 | | 250 Kilometers |

Quebec ★

Saskatchewan

"From Many Peoples Strength"

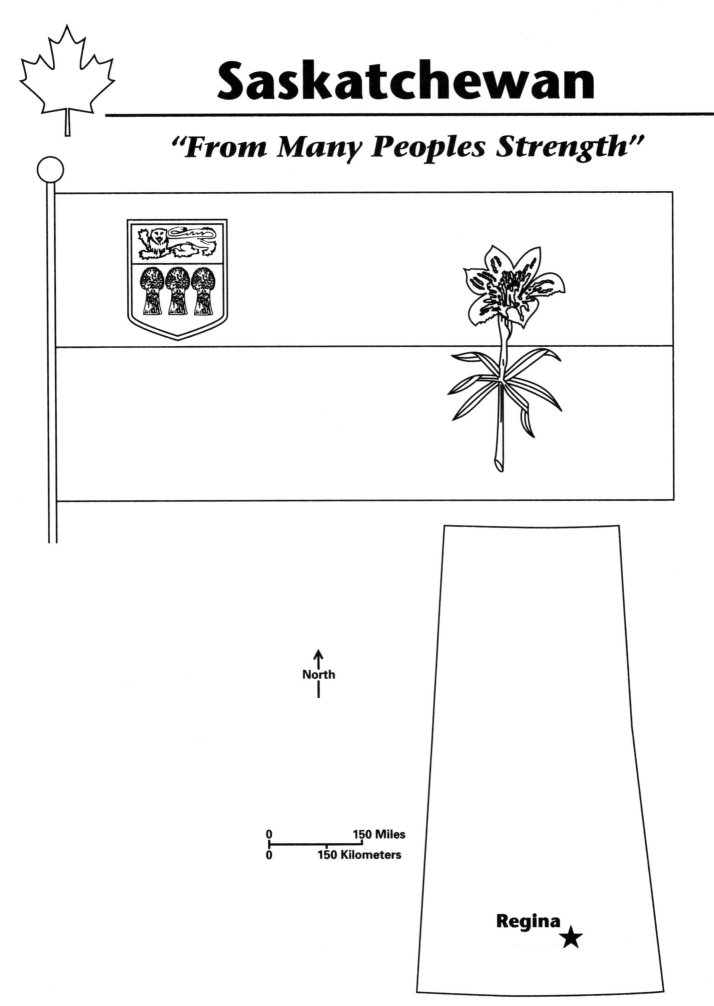

North

0 — 150 Miles
0 — 150 Kilometers

Regina ★

Yukon Territory

(no motto)

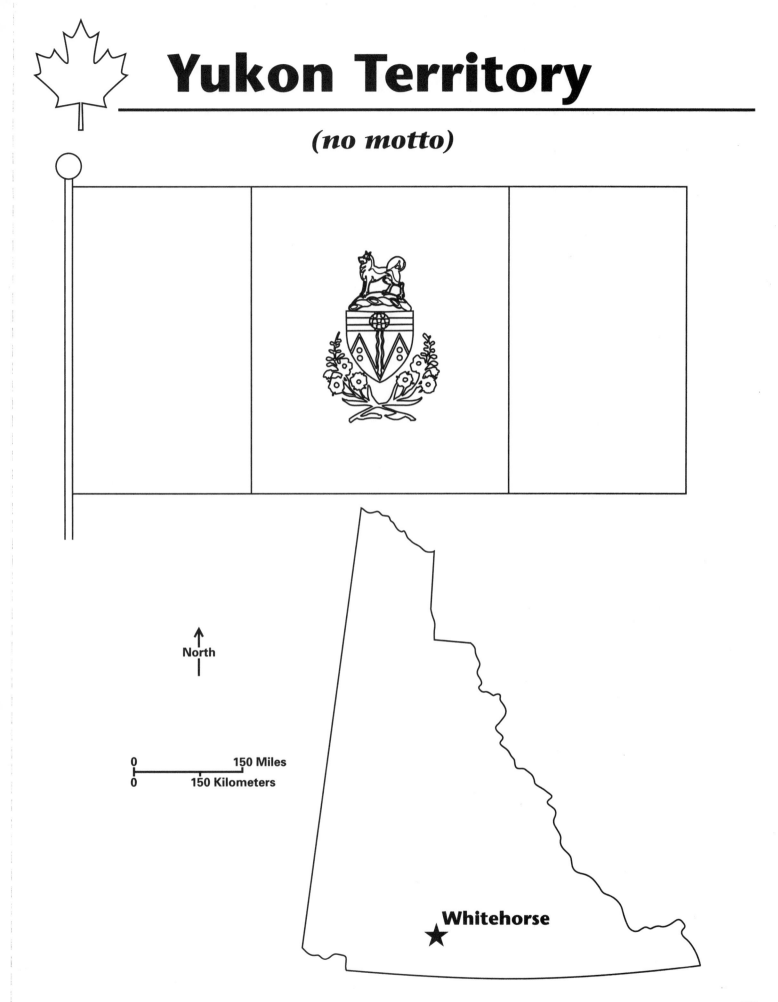

North

0 ——————— 150 Miles
0 ——————— 150 Kilometers

★ **Whitehorse**

79

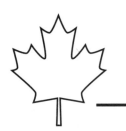

Crossword Puzzle

Provinces and Territories

ACROSS

1. Which province has the capital of Winnipeg?
3. Which part of Canada is the farthest south?
6. Which part of Canada has the capital of Halifax?
8. Which province comes first alphabetically?
10. Which part of Canada has the longest name?
11. Which province is the farthest east?
12. Which province has the capital of Fredericton?

DOWN

2. Which province is on the Pacific coast?
4. Which part of Canada is the farthest west?
5. Which is the smallest province?
7. Which province is made of four straight sides?
9. Which part of Canada has the shortest name?
10. Which part of Canada has the most islands?